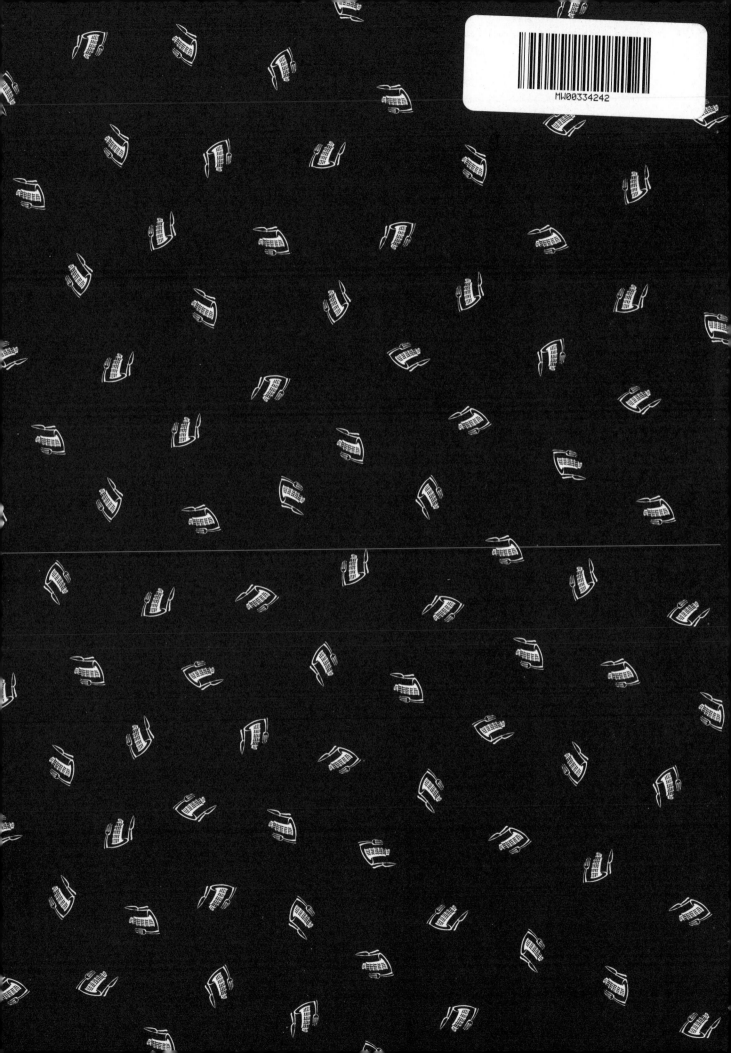

ITALY

CUISINES OF THE WORLD
ITALY

MIRANDA ALBERTI

Food photography: Michael Brauner

THUNDER BAY
P·R·E·S·S

Valle d'Aosta, Piedmont and Lombardy

Venetia and Emilia-Romagna

Liguria and Tuscany

Umbria and the Marches

Lazio and Campania

Abruzzi and Molise

Apulia, Calabria and Basilicata

Sicily and Sardinia

Valle d'Aosta

Lombardy

Trentino-Alto Adige

Veneto

Friuli-Venezia Giulia

Piedmont

Liguria

Emilia-Romagna

Tuscany

Marches

Umbria

Abruzzi

Lazio

Molise

Campania

Apulia

Basilicata

Sardinia

Calabria

Sicily

CONTENTS

ITALY: A CULTURAL AND CULINARY EXPERIENCE

Italy, the land of lemon trees, the land of the classical cultures of Antiquity and where the Renaissance first saw the light of day. This is Italy, a land of bountiful treasures, from olives ripening in the Mediterranean sun to the architectural splendors of Florence and Venice. Its landscapes range from the high, cold lakes of the Alps to sun-drenched beaches, from forests to fertile plains. Its towns are open-air museums. It is hardly surprising that its people have a reputation for enjoying life to the fullest – at home, in the country-side, in the villages, and on the streets of their towns and cities. Nothing expresses this lively enjoyment better than the exuberant diversity of Italian cuisine.

A trip to Italy is a unique culinary experience. Few countries have such a wide range of delicious dishes to offer, partly because each region has its own particular traditional specialties. Dishes reflect the local character and culture, rural or urban, rich or poor, mountain or coastal. In the Tuscan countryside, for example, food tends to be simple and plain; in the great cities, on the other hand, the cooking is usually more elaborate and sophisticated.

This book reflects the extraordinary variety of Italian cuisine. Following an introduction to the country, the people, and the influences that have shaped the cuisine, the recipe sections are listed in the order in which they would appear on a menu, from *anti-pasti*, or starters, to *dolci*, or desserts.

Famous classic dishes appear along-side authentic versions of less familiar, traditional ones. There are notes on some of the most important ingredients, and step-by-step photographs to illustrate some of the more complicated techniques. In many cases, particular wines are recommended to complement particular dishes. There is also a section that offers carefully planned complete menus for different occasions, so you can treat your family and guests to Italian *arte culinaria* at its very best. Finally, a useful glossary explains some less familiar terms and ingredients, including words and expressions used in Italian cooking.

A RICH AND DIVERSE LAND

Over the centuries, Italy's turbulent history has left its mark not only on the social and cultural life of the people, but also on the food they eat. Italian cuisine originated with the early Greeks and Etruscans; later, the expansion of Rome and trade with a widening empire resulted in diverse foreign influences on the Roman cuisine. Then, as the Roman Empire declined, successive invaders introduced more new ingredients to enrich the menu.

By the end of the Middle Ages, the ships of the seafaring republics of Venice and Genoa were bringing back exotic spices and cooking techniques from all over the known world. Italian culinary art reached its zenith during the Renaissance. The Medicis loved fine food, and their cooks created exquisite dishes for them. When Catherine de Medici married Henri II of France, Italian invention spread to French cooking.

Until the mid-19th century, Italy was divided into a host of politically independent city-states and regions, even the smallest of which had its own history, its unique landscape, and, of course, its own distinctive, traditional cuisine. Despite the unification of Italy in 1861, people today still identify strongly with their native region, regarding themselves as Venetian, Piedmontese, Calabrian, Roman, or Sicilian.

Besides this complex history, Italy's landscape and agricultural diversity have played a major role in shaping culinary traditions. In the north, for example, where there is good grazing land, butter is used for cooking. In the rest of Italy, where olive trees abound, food is cooked in olive oil. Tomatoes were first brought to southern Italy from the New World and are particularly important in southern cooking, especially in the creation of the Neapolitan pizza. But it was a long time before pomidori, or "golden apples," found their way to the northern, mountainous regions.

The stark contrast between the industrialized north and the poorer, less-developed south is reflected in both lifestyle and nutrition. And since necessity is the mother of invention, barren regions such as Calabria are also the home of especially imaginative dishes made from simple ingredients, whereas the cuisine of the wealthier north is more lavish.

Over the years, the north-south divide, regional independence, and historical traditions, together with such factors as the landscape and climate, have all contributed to the development of an incomparably rich and varied cuisine, one that is justifiably renowned worldwide.

The tiny island of San Giulio rises from the waters of Lake Orta, which is only just over half a mile wide. An ancient basilica and a seminary testify to the island's religious serenity, which makes it a popular destination for visitors to the Italian lakes.

Valle d'Aosta, Piedmont, and Lombardy

The landscape of northwestern Italy is one of contrasts. The Valle d'Aosta is typified by secluded valleys, glaciers more than 10,000 feet above sea level, and the towering peaks of Mont Blanc, the Matterhorn, Monte Rosa, and Gran Paradiso. The region is rich in Roman ruins, medieval fortresses, picturesque mountain villages, and famous skiing resorts.

Piedmont – literally "at the foot of the mountain" – is enclosed on three sides by the Alps and opens onto the flatlands of Novara and Vercello to the east. Italy's mightiest river, the Po, rises in the mountains and flows through Turin, Piedmont's capital, toward Lombardy and the rice paddies of the Po Valley. To the north lie the beautiful lakes of Maggiore and Orta. The clear rivers and mountain streams provide excellent trout-fishing, while the south of the

region produces some fine wines.

Northern Lombardy, too, lies in the shadow of the Alps. South of the mountains, there are the lakes of Como, Iseo, Idro, and Varese, a popular vacation area renowned for subtropical flora and idyllic landscapes. Milan, Lombardy's capital, is an international commercial, design, and fashion center. The Milanese are justly proud of the Gothic cathedral that dominates the main city square, the Scala opera house, and the elegant Galleria Vittorio Emanuele II shopping arcade.

Valle d'Aosta

Alpine cooking is as varied as the mountain landscape itself. Each valley has its own tradition and its own special dishes. In the past, the people had to make do with the relatively meager produce of the mountains. The staple was polenta, a mush made of cornmeal or buckwheat, often enriched with mushrooms, cheese, or game. The diet also included home-baked bread, garden vegetables, butter, milk, smoked ham, and wine. For today's visitor, edible souvenirs include many varieties of sausage and other air-dried meat products, and a range of famous cheeses such as mild *fontina*, ideal for broiling or baking; the sharper tasting *toma*; and the cake-shaped *robiola*, made from sheep's milk.

Piedmont

From the 15th through the 19th centuries, Piedmont was ruled by the French House of Savoy, and French influence is still evident in its stylish cuisine. Characteristic local dishes include *Bollito misto*, mixed boiled meats, and *Bagna cauda*, a vegetable fondue with hot anchovy and garlic sauce. Game and poultry are traditionally braised in the local red wine. The countryside has its own riches. In summer, the woods abound in wild strawberries; in fall in wild mushrooms as well as the most sought after delicacy of all is the white truffle from the hills around the small town of Alba.

Lombardy

A variety of influences has left Lombardy without on overall regional style of cookery. Instead, its nine provinces have developed their own traditions. However, all have their cooking method in common. dishes are simmered slowly and cooked with butter. Typical specialties include soups, rice dishes, and homemade ravioli; polenta is usually served as a side dish. Milan is the home of *Osso-buco*, braised slices of veal knuckle, often served with a saffron-flavored rice

dish, *Risotto alla milanese*. *Panettone*, a light yeast cake, is sold in a range of sizes. Other cities with their own specialties include Cremona, famous for the manufacture of violins, which produces *torrone*, sticks of almond and honey nougat; and *mostarda*, candied fruits in mustard syrup. Varese produces *amaretti*, tiny macaroons of sweet and bitter almonds. Lombardy cheeses are world-famous, from the sharp *Gorgonzola*, creamy *mascarpone*, mild *Bel Paese*, and strong *taleggio* from Bergamo.

Wines

Valle d'Aosta is a small wine-producing region, whose reds and whites are full of character. Piedmont's main vine-yards are in the south of the region, around Monferrato and in the Langhe hills. They yield fine reds – Barolo, Barbaresco, Barbera, Dolcetto d'Alba, Grignolino – and whites such as Favorita and Cortese di Gavi. The best known of Piedmont's sparkling wines is Asti Spumante.

Lombardy's most important wine-growing areas are Valtellina – home to classic reds such as Sassella, Grumello, and Inferno – and Oltrepò Pavese, which produces white Rieslings, Pinot Bianco, and Cortese; and red Barbera and Bonarda. Outside these areas, fine wines also come from the area west of Lake Garda: Lugana (white), Chiaretto (rosé), and Riviera del Garda (red and rosé). One of Lombardy's most famous drinks is the apéritif Campari, which was created in Milan, while an excellent finishing touch to a meal is grappa, a fiery spirit distilled across all northern Italy from the fermented residue of grapes after pressing.

A forest of pinnacles and statues adorns Milan's vast cathedral, which holds more than 20,000 people. Built over 500 years, from the 14th century onward, the edifice is a triumph of Gothic architecture.

In the fall and winter, roast chestnuts sold by street vendors are a popular Milanese snack.

Venetia

The northeast of Italy boasts a landscape as dramatic as its history. It was once the hinterland of the republic of Venice, and at various periods different parts have belonged to Austria and Yugoslavia. The area consists of three regions – Trentino-Alto Adige, Veneto and Friuli-Venezia Giulia – often simply referred to as Venetia. Its hallmarks are cities, mountains, and water, with the rugged peaks of the Dolomites and the fast-flowing rivers of the fertile valleys of South Tyrol and the leisurely River Po flowing toward the Adriatic. Among the magnificent cities are romantic Verona; Vicenza, birthplace of the architect Palladio; Padua, where villas line the Brenta canal; the seaport of Trieste; and, of course, Venice itself.

The Alpine part of this region borders on Austria and Switzerland, and northern influences have played an important role in molding its culture, character and cuisine. In the fall, the people of the South Tyrol and Trentino celebrate Törggelen, a wine festival that includes lots of hot chestnuts and fresh walnuts. The festivals of the lowlands include the Venice Carnival, held to mark the start of Lent which is celebrated by donning elaborate masks and costumes, and the September Regatta on the Grand Canal, which is no less spectacular.

Trentino and Friuli

Venetia's Alpine region once belonged to Austria, as shown by the presence of dumplings and pastries on local menus. Favorites from Trentino include spinach gnocchi, potato gnocchi, and

Pasta e fagioli, a pasta and bean soup. Polenta is eaten everywhere here. In the area around Trieste, Friuli's culinary tradition shows a strong Slovenian influence. A distinctive local delicacy, *prosciutto di San Daniele*, raw cured ham, is pressed between two wooden planks of fir or pine in order to give it its traditional violin shape.

Veneto

Rice from the Po Valley has always been an essential ingredient in Venetian cooking. So important was it that a dish of rice and young peas – *Risi e bisi* in the Venetian dialect – was traditionally served to the Doge, the head of the Venetian Republic, in a ceremony on the feast day of St. Mark, the city's patron saint. Saffron and other exotic spices were introduced into the kitchen during the Republic's centuries of maritime trade with the Balkans and the Orient.

The sea also has a more direct influence on the Venetian menu. There is a rich selection of fish. *Insalata di frutti di mare*, a popular appetizer, is a delicious mix of squid, mussels, and other seafood; and *baccalà*, dried salt cod, is a typical delicacy. Meat dishes include *Fegato alla veneziana*, named after the city, which consists of calf's liver fried with onions; and *Carpaccio*, raw, marinated fillet of beef, reputedly created in honor of the famous 15th-century Venetian artist Vittore Carpaccio.

Wine

Most of the wines from South Tyrol are red. Mozart's Don Giovanni extolled the virtues of red Marzemino from Trentino's Lagarina Valley, but

Teroldego Rotaliano from Trentino-Alto Adige is king of the region's wines. Wines from east of Lake Garda, such as Tocai del Garda, are light and easy to drink. The limestone soil of Friuli, one of the best wine regions of Italy, produces Picolit, Pinot Grigio, Refosco, Verduzzo, Tocai, and Sauvignon friulano, as well as an excellent grappa. The Venetians' favorite wines are white Tocai, Lugana, and Prosecco. Soave, red Bardolino, and Valpolicella are among Italy's best-known wines.

Emilia-Romagna

Emilia-Romagna is one of Italy's most fertile areas, thanks to the alluvial plains of the Po Delta and the slopes of the Apennines. The main cities are Ravenna with its famed mosaics; Ferrara, city of palaces; and Bologna,

The sunlit town of Malcesine glows against the backdrop of Lake Garda and the Trentino mountains. Sheltered by the Alps, the lake enjoys a Mediterranean climate, and citrus fruits, vines, and olives are grown on its shores.

the culinary capital. The land here is covered with orchards, truck-farms, and chestnut woods, and the cuisine is correspondingly rich. No region is home to more pasta dishes: *Lasagne al forno*, *Tagliatelle al ragù*, *agnolotti*, *cappelletti*, *ravioli*, and at Christmas, mountains of *tortellini*. Pork is an important part of local cooking. Bologna produces *mortadella* sausage, and in the province of Parma delicate Parma ham is left to mature in the fragrant air for a whole year. *Coppa*, from Piacenza, is neck of pork, again air cured; *pancetta*, belly of pork, is used for rendering; and *zampone*, stuffed pig's feet served with lentils, are traditional Christmas fare in Modena. Kid, rabbit, and chicken are also eaten, mainly in stews. Fish from the Adriatic includes red mullet, gray

mullet, sole, swordfish, and squid; the hearty *brodetto* is a worthy rival to the fish soups of other coastal regions. Parma and Reggio are famous for *Parmigiano reggiano*, or Parmesan, a sharp hard cheese made from cow's milk. It is sold in rounds weighing 53 pounds and left to ripen for two to three years. Modena is well-known for *aceto balsamico*, an intense and well-matured balsamic wine vinegar.

Wines
The most popular wines of Emilia-Romagna include white Albana di Romagna, Pinot Bianco, and Trebbiano Romagnolo, or sparkling red Lambrusco di Sorbara, Barbera, Sangiovese di Romagna, and Gutturnio.

Liguria and Tuscany

Liguria is on the French border at the top of the boot of Italy. The region extends in a curve along the edge of the Ligurian Sea from the Riviera di Ponente with its abundant flowers; along the bay of La Spezia; through the capital of Genoa with its proud maritime tradition; and on to the Riviera di Levante. Along the coast, mountains sweep down to the sea. The picturesque villages of the Cinque Terre cling to the cliffs like eagles' nests, and grapevines crowd the terraced vineyards. Inland, there are chestnut woods, fortified mountain villages, perilous passes, castles, and ancient oil presses.

To the south, in Tuscany, is the third riviera, Versilia, bordered by the Appenines and home to the marble quarries of Carrara. Behind the beaches to the south, vegetables and olives are cultivated on a large scale.

Tuscany, the heart of Italy, is one of the world's treasure-houses of culture.

Florence, city of Michelangelo and the Medici, nestles in a silvery, olive-green landscape of vineyards and cypresses. In medieval Siena, the exciting and colorful horserace known as the Palio takes place annually in one of the world's most beautiful squares, the Piazza del Campo. Pisa is famous for its leaning tower, while towns such as Arezzo, Lucca, San Gimignano, and Volterra have hardly changed since the Middle Ages.

The people are characteristic of their regions. The Ligurian coast dwellers have a reputation for being cosmopolitan, thanks to their descent from bold seafarers and traders who traveled widely in the medieval world. By contrast, Ligurians farther inland are considered more reticent and cautious. And the Tuscans, an energetic, practical people, inherit their love of good food from the Etruscans, their ancient ancestors.

Liguria

The mainstays of Ligurian cookery are fish, olives, vegetables, and fresh herbs. The sea is the principal source of food, providing red mullet, anchovies, sardines, and shellfish. Pesto, the famous green sauce made from basil, pine nuts, olive oil, garlic, and pecorino cheese, is the classic accompaniment to minestrone soup or trenette pasta. *Sugo di noci*, a creamy walnut sauce, is served with rigatoni or *pansot* – triangular ravioli filled with wild herbs and ricotta cheese. Typical pasta dishes include *Ravioli al burro*, ravioli with a filling of spinach, ricotta and herbs, swimming in melted sage butter. Another specialty is *cappon magro*, a pyramid of cooked fish and vegetables.

Color-coordinated umbrellas give a Ligurian beach a typically chic Italian style. The picturesque Riviera, which comprises sandy beaches and rocky cliffs, has long been a popular tourist area.

Tuscany

Tuscan cooking is healthy and relatively simple, based on the finest ingredients, especially fresh herbs and young vegetables. Chestnuts, mushrooms, and game are found in the woodlands of the Appenines. The delicious *Lepre in umido*, a ragout of hare, originated in Arezzo. Other Italians call the Tuscans *mangiafagiol*, "bean eaters"; the Tuscans invented *Fagioli all'ucceletto*, beans prepared with tomatoes and sage, and beans such as dried cannellini are added to soups, risottos, and pasta. In Florence, fresh or dried white beans are a favorite accompaniment to meat dishes. Unsalted Tuscan bread is good with a glass of Chianti. Alternatively, there are many varieties of focaccia, a flatbread made with oil or butter, seasoned with herbs or other flavorings and sprinkled with coarse-grained salt. On the coast, the influence of the sea is evident. The best *cacciucco*, a thick fish soup, comes from Viareggio and Livorno.

Wines

Ligurian white wines, such as Vermentino, are drunk in the area around Genoa; the reliable Cinque Terre whites are popular, but the less well known Sciacchetrà dessert wine is well worth trying. Napoleon was impressed with red Rossese di Dolceacqua.

Tuscany's finest white wines are Galestro and Vernaccia di San Gimignano. Among the great reds of the renowned Chianti region are those from Chianti Classico. The heavy clay soil of southern Tuscany also produces fine grapes for reds such as Vino Nobile di Montepulciano and Brunello di Montalcino – one of the great wines of Italy. The renowned dessert wine Vin Santo is made from grapes left to dry out on the vine and intensify in flavor at the end of the season.

Gently rolling hills, scattered pines and cypresses, here and there an ancient farmstead — these are the familiar images of Tuscany, Italy's best-known region.

In summer, poppy fields in full bloom are characteristic of the dazzling colors of the fertile Umbrian landscape.

Umbria and the Marches

Umbria is a largely green and fertile land stretching across the western Apennines. Even today, one can find unspoiled scenes reminiscent of the backgrounds of Giotto's 13th-century frescoes of the life of St. Francis in the church at Assisi. The beautiful valleys are fringed with oak woods in whose soil lie buried the coveted black truffles. Between the woodlands lie olive groves, wheat fields, and tobacco plantations. Ancient castles and medieval hill towns, preserved in their original state, dot the landscape. Sweet chestnuts flourish in the highlands, some 4,000 feet above sea level. Chestnut all-purpose flour is used to make *castagnaccio*, chestnut cake.

The chief fascination of the Marches, which comprise the eastern Apennines and the Adriatic coast, is their picturesque towns such as Ascoli Piceno, Loreto, and Urbino. At lower altitudes, the gently rolling hills are clad with olive groves.

Umbrian farmers enjoy good food and many Umbrians live off the land. The people of the Marches, on the other hand, where the land is mainly mountainous and the soil generally yields poor crops, have long enjoyed a reputation as skilled craftsmen.

Umbria

Umbria is a center for religious festivals and pilgrimages. The town of Gubbio hosts two medieval festivals: the *Corsa dei Ceri*, in which runners compete with giant candles on May 15, and the *Palio della Balestra*, a crossbow contest held in period costume on the last Sunday in May.

The medieval hillside town of Spoleto, one of Italy's most important towns until the eighth century, is renowned for the 20th-century *Festival dei Due Mondi*, a festival of music and drama, which takes place in June or July. In Bastia, suckling pigs are roasted on a spit during the *Sagra della Porchetta* in September. In fall and winter, Spello celebrates the olive festival and the Bruschetta festival, when toasted bread with olive oil and garlic is served.

On these local feast days, every town or village bakes its own special pastries. Other specialties of the region include delicious chocolates called *baci* – Italian for kisses – which are produced in the Umbrian capital and old university town of Perugia. Farther north, at the Abbey of Camaldoli, deep in the dense chestnut woods, the monks sell their distilled herb liqueurs.

Besides its candies, Umbria is also famous for pork and black truffles, the best of both coming from the area around Norcia, birthplace of St. Benedict, the father of Western monasticism. Norcia's acorn-fed hogs produce not only *porchetta*, whole roast suckling pig, stuffed with fennel, garlic, rosemary, and bay leaves and spiced with nutmeg and coriander, but also specialties such as *cotechino*, a spicy pork sausage, and *capocollo umbro*, loin of pork marinated in wine and air-dried.

Lamb, veal, walnut-fed poultry, squab, and fish are also popular and, from November to March, small, black pigs are used to hunt the precious black truffles.

The Marches

For a thousand year the Marches formed the boundary protecting the northeastern flank of the Papal States. It is a region of rich cookery and, like Umbria, it is famed for pork dishes, from suckling pig to such delicacies as *coppa marchigiana*, sausages flavored with almonds, pine nuts, and orange peel; and the peppery *salame di Montefeltro*.

The region is also known for a dish peculiar to Ascoli Piceno, *olive farcite*,

which are large olives stuffed with forcemeat and fried. Along the Adriatic coast, between Ancona and Termoli, hearty fish dishes are popular, especially *brodetto* (fish soup) in dozens of variations, flavored with garlic and herbs.

Wine

Umbria's best-known wine is Orvieto, produced in the region around the city of the same name, which is famous for the impressive façade of its cathedral. Colli del Trasimeno Bianco and the pomegranate-red Rosso come from the shores of Lake Trasimeno.

Wines from the Marches include white Verdicchio, the best of which is made in the Jesi district, Bianco Piceno and Rosso Piceno. A darker, fuller-bodied red, Rosso del Cònero, comes from the steep slopes of Monte Cònero; while Macerata produces the sparkling red Vernaccia di Serrapetrona.

The black-and-white marble fa ade of the cathedral dominates an Orvieto street. The 13th-century cathedral, one of Italy's most famous, contains beautiful frescoes.

Hams and sausages hang above a butcher's counter. Local pork specialties such as pancetta and cotechino are enjoyed far beyond Umbria s borders.

Abruzzi and Molise

The Abruzzi in central Italy is bordered by the Adriatic in the east and the mountain peaks of the Apennines in the west, separated only by a narrow band of hills. Between the sea and the Gran Sasso, the highest and snowiest summit in the Apennines, nature survives undisturbed in vast, lonely forests. The Parco Nazionale d'Abruzzo nature reserve in the south of the region contains many rare animals, including brown bears, foxes, chamois, snow geese, wild cats, and even wolves. Mountain villages, virtually unchanged since the Middle Ages, cling to the sheer mountain slopes.

Farther south is Molise, a truly poor and primitive countryside, in which gently undulating hills alternate with the towering peaks of the Matese and Maiella ranges of the Apennines. As far as the eye can see, there are beautiful, almost forgotten stretches of country-side, broken here and there by solitary pines, evergreen oaks, and cypresses, while olive, fruit, and nut trees spring up amid the evergreen scrubland. Thanks to the harsh conditions, the ancient farmlands have remained immune to outside influences and look much as they always have.

Both the Abruzzese and the inhabitants of Molise are descended from the Samnites, a rugged ancient people who fought against the Roman Empire; but whereas the Abruzzese have a reputation for being warm-hearted, the people of Molise are considered tougher and more calculating. For centuries, the rural way of life has changed as little as the landscape. Sheep-rearing and working

the barren soil are the only resources, and the standard of living is modest.

As a result, the fruits of nature and the labors of the farmers inspire many local festivals. There are celebrations for piglets, for cheese, for artichokes, and for fish. A thrilling annual event, the *Processione dei serpari*, takes place in Cocullo on the first Thursday in May. The statue of St. Dominic, founder of the Dominican order, is carried through the streets with live snakes writhing about it. To celebrate this feast day, the bakeries sell *cervone* and *serpente*, snake-like, serpentine pastries. On Whit Monday, a child dressed as an angel rides on the Pentecost oxen in front of the church in Loreto Aprutino. To mark the Isernia onion fair on June 28 and 29, decoratively braided strands of onions and garlic are sold. Montenero Valcocchiara, in the mountains north of Isernia, holds a rodeo on the first Sunday after August 15, in which competitors ride unbroken horses.

The people of Abruzzi and Molise love to eat, and their everyday fare is lavish as is the festival food. The cuisine is substantial – lard is used for frying – and extremely hot and spicy. Not for nothing is the local peperoncini, a chili pepper, a ubiquitous ingredient in the dishes of the area, referred to as the *diavolillo* or "little devil." Pigs kept in the mountains provide the meat for *prosciutto crudo*, raw, air-dried ham; *pancetta*, smoked belly of pork; smoked neck of pork, and many kinds of sausage and other meat products. *Fegato pazzo* is liver sausage seasoned with chilies; *fegato dolce* is a variation flavored with honey, pistachios, and candied orange

peel. *Porchetta*, or roast suckling pig, makes a highly seasoned and hearty dish. Lamb is also popular, and appears in every imaginable form. The local brodetto is spiced with saffron from L'Aquila, the capital of Abruzzi. Throughout the region, restaurants serve *maccheroni alla chitarra*. This is a local spaghetti-like pasta, made by pressing the dough through a wooden frame strung like a guitar – hence the name – with closely spaced wires.

There are a number of local cheeses. Sheep's milk is the basis for *ricotta*, *mozzarella*, *scamorza* – available fresh or smoked – and *pecorino*. *Mozzarella d'Abruzzo* is sold fresh at farmhouses bearing the sign *caseifici*, "cheese factory"; the little balls of cheese do not keep for long, but they are delicious. Gabriele D'Annunzio, one of Italy's most famous modern writers and a native of Pescara in the Abruzzi, said of *pecorino* that it encapsulated "the whole flavor of

Scattered settlements are characteristic of the foothills of the Monte Sibellini, a range of the Apennines. Little known outside Italy, the plateaux of these blue mountains are havens of undisturbed nature.

the Maiella", the rugged Apennine range south of his home town.

Wine

Montepulciano and Trebbiano grapes, which flourish in both Abruzzi and Molise, produce good, strong wines. The classic red Montepulciano comes from Abruzzi. Trebbiano is a light, dry white wine, which should be drunk young. There is also a strong liqueur called Centerbe, which is distilled from a hundred herbs.

The rigors of farming the unyielding soil of Molise are etched in the faces of its inhabitants.

A monk sits absorbed in his book in the majolica-tiled cloister of Santa Chiara, a peaceful oasis in the hustle and bustle of Naples.

Lazio and Campania

Lazio's fertile western coast is washed by the Tyrrhenian Sea. In the hills of the hinterland, lush pastures are scattered with olive groves. The Apennines to the east and numerous lakes and thermal spas make the area an attractive vacation destination. Rome, capital of the region and of the country, has evolved its own culinary traditions, thanks to the Romans' traditional talent for improvisation. Dishes *alla romana* are elegant but simple and satisfying – and highly seasoned. Roman cuisine is as colorful as the city's inhabitants, who are drawn from all over Italy. Agricultural produce for the city's consumers comes from the surrounding countryside, which is renowned for its vegetables.

Campania, the epitome of the sunny south, takes in the Bay of Naples, the Amalfi coast, the islands of Ischia, Capri, and Procida and the Sorrento peninsula. Wine, olives, cereals, vegetables, and fruits have enriched the local diet since ancient times, as well as bounty from the sea – red mullet, swordfish, sardines, and anchovies. Buffalo, which can still be seen grazing in the meadows, provide the milk used to make creamy white *mozzarella di bufala* cheese.

Naples, the regional capital, is the economic center and gastronomic capital of southern Italy.

Lazio

Lazio, with Rome as its focal point, is where the first known European cookery book and the first true European cuisine both emerged. The citizens of ancient Rome ate dishes ranging from a simple grain mush – the ancestor of polenta – to such exotica as peacocks and dormice. The foods of the Empire included 13 varieties of cheese, a number of wines, and several elaborate desserts. Centuries later, during the Renaissance, the rich and inventive preparations that characterize Roman cooking today developed to its fullest. The results are such favorites of latter-day Romans as *Fettucine al burro*, homemade ribbon pasta served with lots of butter and Parmesan cheese. Other pasta dishes include meat-filled cannelloni, the well-known *Spaghetti alla carbonara* and *Penne all'arrabbiata*, pasta nibs with red chili peppers. A particular specialty is *Saltimbocca alla romana*, thin scallops of veal with ham and sage.

In this region, every festival or holy day has its culinary specialty: After the prayers comes the pleasure, as the celebrants eat, drink, sing, and dance. Lamb and kid are eaten at Easter, while stuffed, spit-roasted sucking pig is the highlight of the *Festa de Noantr* – the Festival of People Like Us – held in the Trastevere district of Rome in mid-July. Stuffed capon is traditional Christmas fare, while lentils with *cotechino* (boiled pork sausage) are enjoyed at the New Year. Between Christmas and January 6, a children's toy market is held in Rome's *Piazza Navona*, at which all kinds of delicious candies are sold.

Campania

Naples' culinary trademark is the Pizza napoletan, made with tomatoes and mozzarella cheese, while semolina or durum wheat pasta is eaten throughout Campania. Olive oil, onions, basil, parsley, and sun-ripened tomatoes make the local sauce that accompanies macaroni, rigatoni, penne, and spaghetti.

Along the coast, this tomato sauce is served with mussels, clams, and squid. A particularly delicious dish from the region is *Fritto misto del golfo*, a crisply deep-fried selection of fish. The specialty of the small island of Ischia in the Gulf of Naples is *Coniglio alla cacciatora*, literally "rabbit hunter-style," made with rabbits fattened on vine leaves and grape pips.

Wine

Dry white Castelli Romani wines are produced in the volcanic soil of Lazio; they include Frascati, Marino, and Colli Albani. The famous Est! Est!! Est!!! comes from Montefiascone. The red wines are more refined, as, for example, Torre Ercolano. The poet Horace sang the praises of Falerno, while Cecubo was a favorite with the Roman emperors Tiberius and Nero.

Campania is not a great wine country. Its whites include Lacrima Christi del Vesuvio, from the slopes of Vesuvius, Greco di Tufo, Capri, Ischia, and Ravello. Taurasi and Solopaca are pleasant, mild reds.

Statues of saints crown Bernini's colonnade around St. Peter's Square in Rome. The 17th-century colonnade, Bernini's masterpiece, guides visitors towards the basilica.

The staples of Calabrian cuisine are summed up in this shop display. Dried tomatoes, tangy tomato paste, black olives, and chilies give the simple country fare its character.

Apulia, Calabria, and Basilicata

The character of the three regions at the foot of Italy derives mainly from their topography. This hot, dry mountainous area includes around 950 miles of coastline and boasts baroque – cities with Romanesque cathedrals, snow-white towns in the Apulian hills, and gray stone villages in the mountains of Calabria.

Highlights for the visitor include Castel del Monte, the 13th-century hunting lodge which belonged to the Holy Roman Emperor Frederick II, and the enchanting Apulian town of Alberobello, whith its *trulli*, whitewashed buildings topped by conical stone roofs. Other attractions include the white chalk cliffs of the Gargano promontory and the ghostly, cave-like dwellings in the rocks of Matera in Basilicata.

Wheat, vegetables, fruit, vines and olives flourish on the fertile plains of Apulia. Calabria produces artichokes, eggplant, tomatoes, and citrus fruits, while in mountainous Basilicata the people wrest the staples of survival – cereals, vegetables, pulses, and olives – from small plots of arid soil.

Since antiquity, this part of Italy has been open to immigrants and invaders, who have left their legacy in the mixed appearance of the population. There are blue-eyed Normans, the darker features of North Africa and the Orient, proud Spaniards, patrician Greeks, and Slavs. Apulia is a moderately prosperous region, but Basilicata and Calabria are for the most part poor, consisting of isolated communities scattered throughout the mountainous and rugged countryside.

In Apulia and Calabria, St. Anthony is honored as the patron saint of pig farmers and St. Anthony's day on January 17 is marked by a huge pig slaughter. In June, there is a swordfish festival in Bagnara near Reggio Calabria; Holy Week is celebrated in Taranto, Apulia, by a 14-hour procession of hooded penitents and flagellants clad in white. In Bari, a ship on wheels is drawn through the city on May 8, to commemorate St. Nicholas, patron saint of sailors and of the city. At Corpus Christi, the archbishop of Brindisi, on horseback and in full regalia, leads a long procession through his city.

Traditional cookery in all three regions is based on durum wheat and olives. The latter, especially, are an important staple. Black olive *baresane*, preserved in brine, are eaten with crusty, saffron-colored bread or *focaccia*, here varied by the addition of olives, pieces of garlic, or dried tomato.

Slightly bitter-tasting onions called *lampasciuni* are pickled and served as an appetizer. The menu also includes a variety of homemade types of pasta, such as ear-shaped *orecchiette*, square *strascenate* or spiral *fusilli*, which are served with mixed vegetables, or with a meat or fish sauce. Lamb, pork, poultry,

Trulli houses make a remarkable roofscape in Alberobello. Unique to Apulia, these gray stone roofs may originate from the local Stone Age culture and reflect the area's lack of timber for building.

and rabbit are the most common meats; beef is served less often. Much use is made of herbs and vegetables from the wild, as in spring lamb braised with wild herbs.

Pizette di patate, pizzas made of potato dough, are popular in Apulia. The Adriatic and Ionian Seas are a rich source of fish, crustaceans, and shellfish. Mussels au gratin, for instance, are a specialty of the Gulf of Taranto, while sea urchins from the waters around Bari are slurped live like oysters and are considered a great treat. In inland Calabria, game dishes are part of the culinary tradition.

Southern Italy is the home of some famous cheeses. The buffalo's milk *mozzarella* from Apulia is regarded as the best in Italy. Cow's milk *provola*, shaped like a ball, and buffalo's milk *scamorza* can be bought fresh, mature, or smoked. Provolone cheese can be made from goat's, sheep's, or cow's milk, and shaped into pears, pigs, people, and other forms before being hung up to

mature; the local variety is called *caciocavallo*. Ricotta is made from sheep's milk and sold as *ricotta fresca* (fresh) or ricotta forte (piquant).

Wine

Apulia offers good white wines, including Locorotondo, Castel del Monte, Martina Franca and Moscato di Trani. Also worth noting are the strong red Salice Salentino and the red and rosé Copertino wines from the Salento peninsula. Among Calabria's most famous wines is Cirò, red, white, and rosé. Basilicata is the home of the fine red wine Aglianico del Vulture.

The Castel del Monte stands sentinel above the Apulian landscape. Built by Holy Roman Emperor Frederick II in 1240 as a hunting lodge, the castle is now one of the region's leading tourist attractions.

A shepherd in Sardinia's Sassari provnce, against the region's barren landscape of brown hillsides and sparse grasslands. Despite the bleakness of the island's uplands, a third of Italy's sheep graze here.

Sicily and Sardinia

As elsewhere, cultural influences and the shape of the land have determined the cuisine of the islands of Sicily and Sardinia where Italian cuisine as we know it today is said to have originated. The Sicilians experimented with the culinary skills of their Greek conquerors, while the Sardinians adopted the tastes of the Phoenicians. Arabian, African, Saracen, Roman, and Norman invaders left behind traces of their culinary as well as their cultural traditions. Due to their isolation from the mainland, the islands each developed in their own unique way.

Sicily is the largest island in the Mediterranean. Lush vegetation flourishes along the sheer mountain slopes of the coast and molten lava still flows from Mount Etna, Europe's largest active volcano. In antiquity, Sicily was

the Romans' grain store, and today more than half the inhabitants still live off the land. The island's colorful history is reflected in the faces of its population. Fair-skinned blondes are almost as common as those with black hair and Middle Eastern features. There are rich remains of Greek, Roman and Norman art.

The *nuraghi*, ancient, circular, tower-like structures of basalt that can be found all over the rocky island, starkly silhouetted against the blue sky, are a unique feature of Sardinia. They are evidence of a forgotten Bronze Age culture, fortresses or villages of a long-lost civilization

Today, Sardinians, mostly shepherds and farmers, live off the land. As in Sicily, fishing for tuna and swordfish plays an important role in the economy, but sheep-breeding is the main source of income and nearly a third of Italy's sheep are to be found on the island. The proud Sardinians still cling to their ancient customs and beliefs, and almost every village has its own dialect.

Festivals are frequent and colorful. At Agrigento, in Sicily, there is an almond blossom festival in February. Almonds also feature at weddings, where the bridal pair are showered with sugared almonds, a symbol of fertility. On June 29, the Feast of St. Peter, the patron saint of fisherman, fish are fried on the streets of fishing villages. On the feast of All Souls, Sicilian children are given cookies called *ossi di morti*, "bones of the dead." On Sardinia, a dangerous horse race called the Ardia takes place at Sedilo in early June and, at the end of October, Aritzo holds a chestnut and hazelnut festival.

Sicilian cookery is based on home-grown produce. The small amount of meat eaten on the island usually takes the form of smoked sausage made from rabbit or pork. Well-known local dishes

include Pasta con le sarde, pasta with sardines, and caponata, a cold vegetable dish made with eggplant. Arancini are fried, stuffed balls of rice about the size of an orange, hence the name. Rice, spices, citrus fruits, and sugar, were all brought to the island by the Arabs.

The Sicilians have created some world-renowned desserts. *Cassata*, a layered cake made with sponge, ricotta cheese, and candied fruits, that is often served at weddings, is also famous as an ice-cream specialty. *Cannoli* are crisp rolls of dough filled with ricotta or farmer cheese; and *frutti di Martorana*, pretty marzipan fruits, are a popular candy.

Sardinian cookery is simple and substantial, and has remained unchanged for centuries. Bread, the mainstay of the islanders' diet, ranges from huge, freshly baked loaves to round, flat, paper-thin pancakes known as *carta di musica*, or sheets of music. Stewlike soups, thick with garden vegetables, are popular. Favorite seasonings include cinnamon, nutmeg, wild fennel, myrtle, rosemary, thyme, bay leaves, and sage. Traditionally, lamb, kid, suckling pig, and game are barbecued on a spit over an open fire of juniper or olive wood. Sardinian cheese is made from sheep's milk; *pecorino sardo* is sold at all stages of maturity.

Wines

The islands offer an ample choice of outstanding wines. Sicily's best white varieties include Regaleali, Corvo bianco, Rapitalà, and Etna Bianco. The fertile black volcanic soil produces excellent red wines – Etna and Cerasuolo – and Marsala is a famous dessert wine. The white wines of Sardinia include the lively Nuragus di Cagliari, and Vernaccia di Oristano, robust and similar to sherry. The heavy, full-bodied red Cannonau and the lighter Monica are produced in various parts of the island.

The riches of the sea make an opulent display of fish and seafood (left) to entice shoppers at a Sicilian market.

ANTIPASTI

Antipasti literally "before the meal" are Italian starters. As dishes that offer wide scope for the imaginative cook, they can be made from almost any ingredient, depending on the season, the occasion, or the dishes to follow. Small delicacies such as *Olive piccanti*, for instance, can be served with apéritifs. *Insalata di frutti di mare* or *Carpaccio* are stylish beginnings to a festive meal. Seasonal vegetables often appear as appetizers and some of them, such as *Insalata di funghi* or *Peperoni all'olio*, can also be used as side dishes. (side dishes that are also eaten as appetizers appear in the chapter on contorni, pages 109 through 123.)

Some antipasti are substantial enough to serve as meals on their own, and these should be followed by the lightest of dishes. Most such starters are bread-based. Among them, a favorite is *Crostini vari*, toasted white bread with toppings ranging from chopped tomatoes and garlic to liver paté. Another is pizza.

For big parties, an *Antipasti assortiti* – a mixed platter of meat, fish, and vegetable appetizers – can easily be assembled at home. This is a familiar offering at Italian restaurants, such a platter, should include some of the famous Italian cured meats from the local delicatessen – salami, mortadella, bresaola, or prosciutto such as Parma or San Daniele ham. These classics are balanced with fruit and vegetable dishes such as figs, melon, olives, artichoke hearts, or mushrooms, according to the season and the cook's fancy.

Peperoni all'olio

Easy • Piedmont **Marinated Sweet Peppers**

4 bell peppers,
(1 red, 1 yellow, 2 green)
1 small bunch parsley (about 1 oz.)
2 garlic cloves
1 small chili pepper (optional • see Glossary)
salt
¾ cup virgin olive oil

Preparation time: 30 minutes
(plus 1 hour marinating time)

500 cal. per serving

1 Light the broiler or preheat the oven to 475 degrees.

2 Wash the bell peppers, wipe them dry, and place under the broiler, turning them at intervals or in the oven for 10 to 12 minutes, until the skins are slightly scorched and blistered. Place in a covered glass bowl, or closed paper bag, until cool enough to handle; the effect of the steam will make the peppers easier to peel.

3 Meanwhile, wash the parsley, shake dry, and chop finely. Peel and mince the garlic. If using the chili pepper, split lengthwise, remove seeds and cut into thin strips. Mix the strips with a little salt and 2 tbsp. olive oil.

4 Peel the sweet peppers using a paring knife. Cut them in half, remove the seeds and ribs, and cut the peppers into ¼-inch strips.

5 Arrange the strips on a serving dish. Include the chili strips, if using (or, of you prefer, hand them round separately). Sprinkle with the chopped garlic and pour on the remainder of the oil. Garnish with the chopped parsley and add salt if required. Leave to marinate in the refrigerator for at least 1 hour.

Olive oil

The cultivation of olives is deeply rooted in Italy's history. For generations, entire regions have made a living from the fruit of the ancient, gnarled, silver-leafed olive trees that are so typical of the Italian landscape.

Although olive trees start to bear fruit after about five years, full production is not reached for 15 to 20 years. Harvesting begins in November. Methods vary, but generally the best olives are picked by hand, and the rest knocked down and caught in nets (above, right). At the oil-mill, the olives are crushed between rotating millstones, then spread on mats and drawn through a cold hydraulic press. The first drops of oil are tested for aroma, consistency, taste, and color, to decide the year's quality. The purest oils, varying in color from green to straw yellow, come from the first cold pressings and are called extra-virgin (the best, most expensive) and virgin. Both give a distinctive and fruity flavor to salads and other – dishes. Later pressings, blended and refined in varying degrees, produce "pure," "extra-fine," and "fine" oils which are lighter in color and flavor and can also be used for frying.

Carpaccio del cipriani

Quick to prepare • Venice **Marinated Fillet of Raw Beef** *Serves 4*

**7 oz. beef fillet in one piece
(or ask butcher to cut into
paper-thin slices)
8 tbsp. virgin olive oil
juice of 2 lemons
½ cup mushrooms
2-oz. piece Parmesan cheese
salt
freshly ground white pepper
1 small bunch of flat-leafed parsley
(¾ oz.)**

**Preparation time: 20 minutes
(plus 1 hour chilling time)**

290 cal. per serving

1 Wrap the beef fillet, if whole, in plastic wrap, and place in the freezer for 1 hour – chilled meat is easier to slice.

2 Using a very sharp knife, cut the chilled fillet into paper-thin slices. Arrange them on a serving dish and pour 4 tbsp. olive oil and half the lemon juice. Cover and leave to marinate for about 15 minutes.

3 Meanwhile, trim the mushrooms, rinse, and drain well. Cut them into thin slices and spread them over the meat. Cut the Parmesan into very thin slices or shavings and arrange on top.

4 Season with salt and pepper, and sprinkle the remainder of the oil and lemon juice over the dish. Wash the parsley and shake it dry. Cut off the leaves and sprinkle them, whole, over the Carpaccio. When serving, put additional olive oil and salt on the table so that guests can season the dish to their taste. Serve with crusty white bread.

Wine: A fresh, light, white wine, such as a Franciacorta Bianco from Lombardy, goes well with this dish.

Insalata di funghi

Simple • Umbria **Mushroom Salad** *Serves 4*

**5 cups mushrooms
juice of 2 lemons
salt
1 bay leaf
7 tbsp. virgin olive oil
freshly ground white pepper
small bunch of parsley (1 oz.)
1 garlic clove
1 chili pepper (optional • see
Glossary)**

**Preparation time: 30 minutes
(plus 2 hours marinating time)**

260 cal. per serving

1 Trim, rinse, and drain the mushrooms. Add half the lemon juice and a little salt to 1 quart of water in a saucepan and bring to the boil. Add the mushrooms and bay leaf and simmer for about 5 minutes.

2 Drain the mushrooms thoroughly on a clean cloth, then pat them dry with kitchen paper. Cut into slices about 1/4 inch thick and place in a serving bowl. Pour the olive oil and remaining lemon juice over them. Season with salt and pepper.

3 Wash the parsley, pat dry, and chop finely. Peel the garlic and cut it into thin slices. If using the chili pepper, halve it lengthwise, remove seeds, and cut into

thin strips. Stir the parsley, garlic, and chili into the mushrooms.

4 Leave the salad to marinate in a cool place (not the refrigerator) for at least 2 hours. It tastes even better if left overnight.

Wine: A light Prosecco Frizzante from Venice is a good accompaniment.

Variation:
Funghi sul crostini
(Mushrooms on Toast)
Bake 8 slices of white bread, ¾ inch thick, as for the crostini on page 32, Step 4. Top each slice with 1 tbsp. of the mushroom salad.

Crostini di fegato di pollo

Hot Chicken Liver Canapés

Not difficult • Tuscany   *Serves 4*

8 fresh chicken livers
1 medium-sized onion
1 carrot
1 stick celery
1 garlic clove
1 medium bunch flat-leafed
parsley (about 2 oz.)
2 tbsp. butter
5 tbsp. virgin olive oil
½ cup dry white wine
salt
freshly ground black pepper
juice of 1 lemon
1 tbsp. capers
1 tsp. anchovy paste
1½ cup meat broth
12 slices crusty white bread
(Tuscan or French bread)

Preparation time: 1½ hours

450 cal. per serving

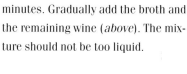

1 Clean the chicken livers carefully, removing any connective tissue and green stains (*above*). Wash and pat dry. Peel and finely chop the onion and carrot. Trim, string, and finely chop the celery. Peel and finely chop the garlic. Wash and dry the parsley. Finely chop half of it and mix with the garlic.

2 In a skillet, heat half the butter with 1 tbsp. olive oil. Gently fry the chopped onion, carrot, and celery. Add the chicken livers, sauté briefly, then pour in half the wine. Let it evaporate, then cover and simmer over medium heat for about 15 minutes. Season with salt and

pepper. Add the parsley-garlic mixture and the lemon juice.

3 Purée the chicken liver mixture in a blender with 1 tsp. capers. Stir in the anchovy paste and return the mixture to the pan. Add the rest of the butter, cover, and simmer gently for about 5

minutes. Gradually add the broth and the remaining wine (*above*). The mixture should not be too liquid.

4 Preheat the oven to 400 degrees. Arrange the slices of bread on a cookie sheet, sprinkle with the remaining olive oil, and bake on the top shelf of the oven for 4 to 5 minutes, until golden-brown. Spread the toasted bread with the liver mixture. Garnish with the rest of the capers and parsley leaves.
Serve hot.

Wine: A deep red Chianti Classico that has been laid down for some time goes well with this dish.

Variation:
Crostini al tonno
(Hot Tuna Canapés)
As an alternative to chicken livers, the toasted bread slices can be spread with a blended mixture of ⅔ cup canned tuna, drained of oil, and 7 tbsp. butter, plus an optional 1 tsp. anchovy paste. Garnish with 2 tsp. capers, a few parsley leaves, and slices of lemon. To complement the tuna, choose a fresh white wine, such as a Tocai from Friuli.

Mozzarella e pomodori

Very quick and easy • Naples

Mozzarella and Tomatoes

Serves 4

4 firm, ripe beefsteak tomatoes
9 oz. mozzarella cheese
salt
1 tsp. dried oregano
fresh basil
freshly ground black pepper
1 tsp. capers
8 black olives
4 tbsp. virgin olive oil

Preparation time: 10 minutes

290 cal. per serving

1 Wash the tomatoes and cut each one into ¼ inch thick slices, discarding the stalk base. Drain the mozzarella well, then cut into thin slices.

2 Arrange alternate slices of tomato and mozzarella in an overlapping pattern on a large, flat serving platter. Season with salt and sprinkle with the oregano.

3 Wash and drain the basil. Decorate the cheese and tomatoes with basil leaves. Sprinkle with freshly ground black pepper.

4 Garnish with the capers and olives and sprinkle with the olive oil. Serve immediately with crusty white bread.

Variation:
Mozzarella al forno
(Baked Mozzarella)
Preheat the oven to 200 degrees. Cut the mozzarella cheese into round slices and lay each one on a slice of crusty white bread. Season with salt, pepper and oregano. Place on a baking tray and sprinkle with olive oil. Bake for 6 to 8 minutes, until the cheese begins to melt. Serve as a starter or snack.

Note: Mozzarella is traditionally made from water-buffalo's milk, but nowadays is more often available made from cow's milk. Buffalo milk cheese has a stronger flavor than the milder, creamier cow's milk.

Olive piccanti

Very quick and easy • Sicily

Spicy Olives

Serves 4

1 cup black olives, pitted
1 stick celery
2 garlic cloves
3 shallots or green onions (scallions)
1 fresh chili pepper (see Glossary)
5 tbsp. virgin olive oil

Preparation time: 10 minutes

330 cal. per serving

1 Dry the olives by patting them with kitchen paper and put them in a bowl.

2 Wash and trim the celery, removing leaves and string. Using only the best 4-inch length, cut it into strips ¼-inch thick. Peel and finely chop the garlic. Peel the shallots or green onions (scallions) and cut them into thin rings. Rinse the chili pepper and remove the stalk. Halve the chili lengthwise with a sharp knife, remove the seeds, and cut it into thin strips.

3 Combine the celery, garlic, and onions with the olives in the bowl. Arrange the chili strips on top of the olives. Pour on the olive oil.

Wine: Serve either and apéritif or a young, light red wine, such as a Valtellina from Lombardy.

Variation:
Olive con buccia d'arancio
(Olives with Orange Peel)
Mix 1¾ cups pitted black olives with 1 tsp. sugar and the grated rind of one untreated orange. Put the mixture in a small cheesecloth bag. Fasten the bag and leave for 3 to 4 days near a heat source, such as a radiator or kitchen stove, shaking from time to time, until the olives have absorbed the orange flavor.

Insalata di frutti di mare

Seafood Salad

Time-consuming ¥ Coastal regions

Serves 4 to 6

*1 lb. 5 oz. fresh baby
octopus, or squid
(or, if unavailable, 14 oz. ready
cleaned fresh or frozen squid)
juice of 3 lemons
3 tbsp. red wine vinegar
salt
2 lb. 2 oz. mussels
1¼ cups bay shrimp in their shells
(optional)
1 small bunch flat-leafed parsley
(about 1 oz.)
3 garlic cloves
1 red chili pepper (see Glossary)
6 tbsp. virgin olive oil*

*Preparation time: 1 hour
(plus 2 hours marinating time)*

*290 cal. per serving
(if serving 6)*

1 To clean baby octopus (*above*) or squid, carefully pull the head plus tentacles away from the body pouch. Remove the pen, or quill, and the ink sac. Sever the head and viscera from the tentacles and discard. Squeeze out the beak from the tentacles and discard. Skin the pouch and wash it thoroughly inside and out under running water.

2 In a saucepan, bring 1 quart water to the boil, together with the juice of 1 lemon, the red wine vinegar, and ½ tsp. salt. Add the pouches and tentacles, cover and cook over medium heat for about 15 to 20 minutes (depending on size) until tender (defrosted frozen squid may take less time.) Leave to cool in the liquid.

3 Scrape the mussels under running water and remove beards with the blunt edge of a knife (*above*). Tap sharply any shells that are open, and if they don't close, discard them. Bring 1 cup water to the boil, add the mussels, cover the pan, and cook over a high heat until the mussels open. Discard any mussels that remain closed. Remove the rest from their shells and sprinkle with the juice of half a lemon.

4 If including shrimp, wash the shrimp in their shells and put them in boiling salted water with the juice of half a lemon. Boil for 5 minutes, strain through a sieve, and leave to cool. Peel off the shells. Make an incision along the back of each shrimp and remove the dark, vein-like intestine. Rinse in lukewarm water.

5 Pour off the liquid from the squid and drain thoroughly. Cut the pouches into thin rings and the tentacles into pieces about ½ inch thick. Mix mussels, shrimp, and squid together in a bowl.

6 Wash the parsley, shake it dry, and mince it. Peel and mince the garlic. Halve the chili pepper lengthwise, remove the seeds, and cut into strips. Stir the parsley, garlic, and chili into the seafood mixture.

7 Sprinkle the seafood with the juice of 1 lemon. Add the olive oil and mix thoroughly. Leave in a cool place (not in the refrigerator) to marinate for at least 2 hours. Serve with crusty white bread.

Wine: A dry white wine, such as a Tocai from the Veneto or a Trebbiano d'Abruzzo, goes well with this dish.

Pizzette di patate

Not difficult · Apulia   **Little Potato Pizzas**   *Serves 4*

1¼ lb. floury potatoes
salt
1 large onion
5½ oz. bacon slices
¾ cup all-purpose flour
1 egg
grated nutmeg
2 tbsp. olive oil
1¾ cups tomatoes, fresh or canned
1 small bunch flat-leafed parsley (about 1 oz.)

Preparation time: 1 hour

430 cal. per serving

1 Peel the potatoes, cut them into quarters, and simmer in a pan of salted water for about 20 minutes.

2 Meanwhile, peel the onion and slice into thin rings. Dice the bacon and put it in a skillet over low heat until it has rendered up some of the fat. Remove the bacon with a slotted spoon and set aside. Sauté the onion in the bacon fat until transparent.

3 Drain the potatoes and, while still warm, either mash them or press them through a sieve onto a floured pastry board; leave to cool. Add the all-purpose flour and egg, and season with salt and a little grated nutmeg. Work 1 tbsp.

olive oil into the potato mixture and knead into a smooth dough. Divide into four and roll each serving into a round 7 inches in diameter and ½ inch thick.

4 Preheat the oven to 425 degrees. Skin and deseed the tomatoes as described on page 41, Step 3, or drain the canned tomatoes. Chop into small pieces. Wash and finely chop the parsley.

5 Place the dough rounds on a lightly oiled baking sheet and top with the bacon, onion, tomatoes and parsley. Season with salt and pepper and bake in the oven for 20 to 25 minutes. Sprinkle with a little oil before serving.

Calzone

Fairly easy · Campania   **Stuffed Pizzas**   *Serves 4*

For the dough:
2 tbsp. fresh yeast or 1 package active dried yeast
pinch of sugar
1¾ cups all-purpose flour
1 tsp. salt ¥ 2 tbsp. olive oil

For the filling:
4 cups mushrooms
1 tbsp. butter
salt ¥ freshly ground pepper
10½ oz. sliced cooked ham
10½ oz. mozzarella cheese
4 tbsp. grated Parmesan cheese
1 tsp. oregano · 4 tbsp. olive oil

Preparation time: 2 hours

880 cal. per serving

1 Make a pizza dough following the recipe on page 41.

2 For the filling, trim the mushrooms, rinse them, pat dry, and cut into thin slices. Melt the butter in a saucepan, add the mushrooms, and sauté over high heat for about 5 minutes, until the liquid has evaporated. Season with salt and pepper, and leave to cool.

3 Cut the ham into thin strips. Drain the mozzarella well, then cut it into small dice. Mix the ham and the mozzarella in a bowl with the grated Parmesan. Add the cooled mushrooms. Season with oregano, salt and pepper.

4 Preheat the oven to 475 degrees. Grease a cookie sheet with a little olive oil. Knead the four portions of dough vigorously and roll out into four thin, flat rounds.

5 Spread a quarter of the filling on one half of each round, leaving the edges clear. Fold the other half over the filling. Press the edges firmly to seal. Arrange the calzone on the baking sheet. Brush each one with 1 tbsp. olive oil and bake in the middle of the oven for about 20 minutes until golden-brown.

Wine: Try a dry red wine such as a Copertino from Apulia.

Pizza "quattro stagioni"

Four Seasons Pizza

More complex • Campania

Serves 4

For the dough:
2 tbsp. fresh yeast or 1 package
active dried yeast
pinch of sugar
1 ¾ cups all-purpose flour
1 tsp. salt
2 tbsp. olive oil

For the topping:
1 ¾ cup tomatoes, fresh or canned
salt
freshly ground black pepper
6 tbsp. virgin olive oil
5 to 6 basil leaves
2 tsp. oregano
10 ½ oz. mozzarella cheese
1 cup broccoli florets
1 red bell pepper
¾ cup mushrooms
4 anchovy fillets canned in oil
1 cup artichoke hearts canned in oil
1 cup seafood salad (see recipe page 36)
10 black olives
1 tbsp. capers

1 In a small bowl, dissolve the yeast and sugar in ½ cup lukewarm water. Stir in 2 to 3 tbsp. of the all-purpose flour to make a smooth paste, lightly dust with a little more all-purpose flour, and leave in a warm place for 15 to 30 minutes. If using dry yeast, follow package directions.

2 Sift the remaining all-purpose flour onto a pastry board, make a well in the center, and pour in the yeast mixture and the salt. Make a dough, gradually adding the oil and about ½ cup lukewarm water, and knead until smooth and elastic. Shape it into a ball, divide into four portions, cover with a damp cloth, and leave to prove in a

warm place for 1½ to 2 hours, until doubled in size.

3 Meanwhile, prepare the topping. Plunge fresh tomatoes briefly in boiling water, skin, halve and remove seeds (*above*). Or, if canned tomatoes, drain them. Chop the tomatoes into small pieces, put them in a bowl, season with salt and pepper, and mix in 3 tbsp. of the olive oil. Wash and dry the basil, chop it finely and add with the oregano to the tomatoes. Drain and dice the mozzarella.

4 Wash and trim the broccoli. Seed and derib the bell pepper and cut it into

strips. Trim, rinse, pat dry and slice the mushrooms. Blanch the broccoli, pepper, and mushrooms separately by simmering them in salted water for 2 to 5 minutes, and drain thoroughly.

5 Place all the topping ingredients to hand in separate bowls. Drain the anchovies. Drain and halve the artichoke hearts. Preheat the oven to 475°F or Mark 9).

6 Lightly oil a cookie sheet. Roll the dough into four pizza rounds and place them on the cookie sheet. Press each one flat with your hands, then make a raised edge all round (*above*).

7 Spread the tomato mixture evenly over the top of the dough. To represent the four seasons, divide each pizza into four sections. Use artichoke hearts for spring, seafood for summer, mushrooms for fall, and broccoli for winter. Then distribute olives, capers, and anchovies over all four sections. Sprinkle with olive oil.

8 Bake the pizzas in the bottom of the oven. After 15 minutes, sprinkle with the diced mozzarella and bake for a further 5 minutes. Serve hot. Put olive oil, salt, and pepper on the table for additional seasoning.

PRIMI PIATTI

F ollowing antipasti on the Italian menu, the first appetizer – the *primo piatto* – consists of soup, pasta, rice, or polenta. The soup could either be a simple clear broth garnished with pasta or egg, or a sustaining vegetable minestrone, for which every housewife has her own special recipe. *Minestroni* are often more like stews than soups, and always taste wonderful.

Risottos are made with round-grain rice – arborio and vialone, for example – and should be moist and tender. Polenta, still a staple in many regions, can be fried in butter or oil, or enhanced, as in *Polenta con tartuffi*, with cheese and truffles. Another popular homemade dish is *gnocchi*, fluffy little balls of dough made from flour, potatoes, cornmeal, or farina, often served with a piquant sauce.

The most frequently served *primo piatto* is pasta. Apart from the well-known spaghetti, fettucine, macaroni, and stuffed pasta such as ravioli, there are countless other forms of pasta, accompanied by a huge range of imaginative sauces. From the *pasta all'uovo* of northern Italy, made with eggs, high-gluten flour, and butter, or the eggless farina (durum wheat) and oil pasta of the south, the variety of shapes and the wealth of delicious pasta dishes is overwhelming.

Minestrone di verdure

Simple • Lombardy   **Minestrone Soup**   *Serves 6 to 8*

2 tbsp. dried cannellini
or navy beans
salt
1 sage leaf
1 leek
3 carrots
½ head savoy cabbage
1 stick celery
3 medium-sized potatoes
1 zucchini
2 ripe tomatoes (plum tomatoes, if
available)
1 tbsp. butter
4 tbsp. olive oil
8 cups meat broth (if fresh broth is
unavailable, use broth cubes)
⅓ cup ditalini, or other short pasta
1 garlic clove
10 to 15 rosemary leaves
1 fresh or dried chili pepper
freshly grated Parmesan cheese

Preparation time: 1 ½ hours
(plus bean-soaking time)

170 cal. per serving
(if serving 8)

1 Soak the beans in cold water for 7 to 8 hours, or overnight. Drain them, then boil them in fresh water for 30 to 45 minutes, adding the sage.

2 Clean the leek and cut it into ¼ inch rings. Peel and slice the carrots. Remove the core from the cabbage and cut it into strips. Trim and string the celery and cut into ¼ inch pieces. Peel and dice the potatoes. Top, tail, and slice the zucchini. Wash and drain all the vegetables. Skin and deseed the tomatoes (page 41, Step 3), and cut into eighths.

3 Heat the butter and half the oil in a large saucepan. Add the leek rings and sauté briefly, stirring constantly. Strain the precooked beans through a sieve,

rinse them under running water and add to the pan. Gradually add the remaining prepared vegetables and cook for about 10 minutes.

4 Add the broth. Cover, and cook over medium heat for 20 to 30 minutes, stirring from time to time. Season with salt. Add the pasta and cook over a low heat until al dente.

5 Meanwhile, peel and slice the garlic. Heat the remaining olive oil in a small skillet, add the garlic, rosemary, and whole chili pepper, and fry them briefly in the oil, taking care not to burn the garlic.

6 Finally, stir the rosemary mixture into the soup. Serve the minestrone hot in a soup tureen, passing the grated Parmesan in a separate bowl.

Variation:
Minestrone con piselli e pesto

(Minestrone with Peas and Pesto) Prepare the soup as above, omitting the rosemary mixture, but adding ⅔ cup freshly shelled, or frozen, peas with the pasta. For the pesto, follow the instructions on page 64, but omit the chili pepper. If the paste is too thick, stir in a little soup liquid. At table, stir a tablespoonful of pesto into each bowl of soup. Serve with toasted slices of white bread rubbed with half a garlic clove.

Wine: If you like to serve wine with soup, try a white Trebbiano di Romagna, or a red Griguolino or Chianti.

Note: There are many variations of this soup. You can add whatever vegetables are handy – mushrooms, onions, green beans, Swiss chard, etc. Tiny bits of lean bacon or ham are also often included

Zuppa alla valdostana

Simple • Valle d Aosta

Cabbage Soup with Bread and Cheese

Serves 4

1 savoy cabbage

salt

8 slices day-old white bread, crusts removed

8 oz. fontina cheese (or Jack cheese, if not available)

⅓ cup butter

about 3 cups beef or chicken broth

freshly ground white pepper

Preparation time: 1½ hours

670 cal. per serving

1 Remove the outer leaves and core of the cabbage, wash and drain it. Cut it into quarters, then into thin strips.

2 Blanch the cabbage strips in 2 cups boiling salted water for about 2 minutes. Rinse with cold water and drain thoroughly. Cut the bread and the cheese into slices. Preheat the oven to 475°F degrees.

3 Grease a large ovenproof dish with 1 tbsp. of the butter. Cover the base with a layer of the bread and moisten with 3 tablespoons of broth. Cover with a layer of cabbage. Cut about 2 tablespoons butter into slivers and scatter on top of the cabbage. Cover with cheese slices.

4 Continue to arrange alternate layers of bread, broth, cabbage, butter, and cheese, ending with a layer of bread slices. Pour the remaining broth over the bread and top with slivers of butter.

5 Bake on the top shelf of the oven for 20 to 30 minutes, until the bread topping is golden-brown. Season with salt and pepper.

Wine: A dry white wine, such as a Soave from the Veneto, goes well with this soup.

Minestra di patate e carote

Not difficult • Trentino

Potato and Carrot Soup

Serves 6 to 8

1¾ cups potatoes

1¾ cups carrots

2 sticks celery

1 large onion

2 tbsp. butter

2 quarts chicken broth

salt

⅓ cup ditalini, or other short pasta

1 garlic clove

4 sage leaves

1 tbsp. virgin olive oil

freshly ground black pepper

6 tbsp. freshly grated Parmesan cheese

Preparation time: 1½ hours

200 cal. per serving (if serving 8)

1 Peel and wash the potatoes and cut into quarters. Peel the carrots and cut into pieces. Remove strings from the celery, wash and cut into pieces ¾ inch long. Peel the onion and chop finely.

2 Melt the butter in a large saucepan, add the onion, and sauté until transparent. Gradually add the potatoes, carrots, and celery. Cover the pan and cook the vegetables in the hot butter, shaking the pan from time to time. Add the broth. Season with salt and cook, covered, over a medium heat for 25 to 30 minutes.

3 With a slotted spoon, remove the vegetables from the broth. Purée them through a sieve or in a food processor and return the purée to the pan.

4 Bring the soup back to the boil, stir to incorporate the purée, then add the pasta, and simmer over low heat until the pasta is al dente.

5 Peel and finely chop the garlic. Wash the sage leaves. Heat the oil in a small skillet, add the garlic and sage, and fry briefly, taking care not to burn the garlic. Stir into the soup, and season with pepper. Serve with the grated Parmesan and, if you like, crusty bread.

Wine: A delicate dry white wine from Friuli, such as a Sauvignon, is an excellent choice.

Arancini di riso

Fried Rice Balls

Makes about 16 arancini

2 cups arborio or other risotto rice

salt

1 pinch powdered saffron

2 eggs

4 tbsp. freshly grated Parmesan cheese

1 small, boned chicken breast

1 small onion

1 small carrot

1 small stick celery

1 small bunch of flat-leafed parsley (about 1 oz.)

⅓ cup mozzarella cheese

3 tbsp. olive oil sunflower or vegetable oil, for frying

1 chili pepper

⅔ cup lean ground beef

6 tbsp. sieved tomatoes

⅓ cup freshly shelled, or frozen, peas

about ¾ cup meat broth

freshly ground white pepper

6 tbsp. fresh bread crumbs

2 tbsp. all-purpose flour

Preparation time: 2 hours

249 cal. per rice ball

1 Bring 5 cups salted water to the boil in a saucepan. Add the rice and cook over a low heat for about 15 minutes, stirring frequently, until the water is absorbed and the rice is tender but still firm. Toward the end of the cooking time, dissolve the saffron in 3 tbsp. hot water and stir into the rice. Whisk 1 egg. Stir it and the grated Parmesan into the rice. Leave to cool.

2 Wash and dry the chicken breast, and cut it into small cubes. Peel the onion, scrub the carrot. Trim, wash, and string the celery. Chop all the vegetables into tiny pieces. Wash the parsley, shake dry and chop finely. Cut the mozzarella into 32 cubes.

3 Heat the olive oil in a heavy pan. Sauté the onion until transparent. Add the carrot, celery, and whole chili pepper and fry briefly. Add half the parsley, the diced chicken, and ground beef, season with salt and sauté for about 5 minutes.

4 Add the sieved tomatoes and the peas. Cover the pan and cook over medium heat for 15 to 20 minutes. As the liquid evaporates, add the broth, a little at a time. Sprinkle the mixture with the best of the chopped parsley and continue to cook, stirring frequently, until the mixture thickens. Remove the chili pepper.

5 Whisk the second egg in a bowl, and lightly season with salt and pepper. Place the bread crumbs on a flat plate.

6 Shape a handful of the rice into a ball. Make a hollow in the center with your index finger. Fill the hollow with the meat and vegetable mixture and 2 cubes of the mozzarella cheese (*above*). Then seal the hollow with a little more rice and roll into a ball. Dust the ball lightly with all-purpose flour. Make 15 more balls in the same way.

7 Dip each rice ball in the beaten egg, roll it in the bread crumbs (*below*) and place it carefully on a plate.

8 In a pan, heat a generous quantity of sunflower oil. Deep-fry the rice balls, a few at a time, until golden. Put them briefly on kitchen paper to drain off surplus oil, then arrange on a warmed serving platter. Serve very hot.

Wine: A dry white wine with a generous bouquet, such as an Etna from Sicily, goes well with arancini.

Risotto nero alla fiorentina

Risotto with Squid

Serves 4

1 ¼ lb. Swiss chard, or spinach or
rocket

salt

1 ¼ lb. squid, or small cuttlefish,
with ink sacs

1 medium-sized onion

1 garlic clove

5 tbsp. virgin olive oil

1 fresh chili pepper

1 cup dry white wine

1 ⅓ cups arborio, or other risotto
rice

1 small bunch of flat-leafed parsley
(1 oz.)

Preparation time: 1 ½ hours

520 cal. per serving

1 Wash the chard and remove the stalks and ribs. If using spinach or rocket, wash, and remove the stems. Bring 2 cups salted water to the boil and blanch the leaves. Drain over a bowl, reserving the cooking water, squeeze the leaves dry, and chop finely.

2 Clean the squid or cuttlefish (page 36, Step 1), reserving the ink sacs. Cut the pouch and tentacles into strips. Mince the onion and garlic.

3 Heat 3 tbsp. of the oil in a heavy pan, and sauté the onion, and garlic until transparent. Add the whole chili and the squid, and sauté until slightly brown. Add the wine and season with salt. Cover and cook over medium heat for about 10 minutes. Add the chard and cook for a few minutes more.

4 Puncture the ink sacs and add the ink to the pan. Cook for a further 10 minutes. (If you wish, remove the chili

pepper at this stage). Stir in the rice, then add a little reserved chard water. Cook for 15 to 20 minutes, stirring continuously and gradually adding the water, until the liquid is absorbed and the rice is tender, but still moist.

5 Wash, dry, and finely chop the parsley and sprinkle over the risotto. Pour over the remaining oil and serve. Wine: Choose a dry white wine, such as a Grave del Friuli or a Ligurian Vermentino, to go with this dish.

Note: Italians mostly use small cuttlefish for this dish but squid are just as good. If using frozen squid, make sure the ink sacs are included.

Risotto ai frutti di mare

Seafood Risotto

3 cups fresh mussels
5 tbsp. olive oil
2 garlic cloves
1 ¾ cups raw shrimp or
1 cup cooked, shelled shrimp
1 ¾ cups fresh, or frozen, squid
1 small onion
½ cup dry white wine
3 tbsp. brandy
1 ¼ cups arborio, or other risotto
rice
salt
freshly ground pepper
1 small bunch of flat-leafed parsley
(1 oz.)

Preparation time 1 ½ hours
620 cal. per serving

1 Clean the mussels as described on page 36, Step 3, making sure all shells are tightly shut. Bring 1 cup water to the boil with 1 tbsp. oil and 1 peeled garlic clove. Add the mussels, cover, and cook over high heat until they open. Discard any that remain closed. Reserve 8 mussels for garnish and shell the rest. Strain the liquid through a fine sieve into a bowl and set aside.

2 If using unshelled shrimp, wash and shell them. Make an incision along the back to remove the dark, vein-like intestine. Clean the squid as described on page 36, Step 1, discarding everything except pouches and tentacles. Cut into strips ½ inch thick.

3 Peel the onion and the second garlic clove, and chop them finely. Heat 3 tbsp. of the oil in a heavy pan, add the onion and garlic, and sauté until transparent.

Add the squid and brown lightly. Pour on the wine, cover, and cook for about 10 minutes, until the wine has evaporated.

4 Meanwhile, in a skillet, heat the remaining 1 tbsp. oil, add the shrimp, and brown lightly. Pour the brandy over the shrimp and simmer for 2 to 4 minutes, depending on size.

5 Add the rice to the onions and squid in the heavy pan. Cook for 15 to 20 minutes, stirring continuously, gradually adding the mussel broth and, when it runs out, hot water. Season with salt and pepper. Finally, add the shrimp and mussels, and simmer for about 5 the rice should be moist, tender but firm.

6 Wash, dry, and chop the parsley. Sprinkle it on the risotto and garnish with the reserved mussels.

Risotto alla milanese

Saffron Risotto

Needs care • Milan

Serves 4

about 1 quart meat broth
1 marrow bone
1 small onion
½ cup butter
1 ¾ cups arborio, or other risotto
rice
½ cup dry white wine
salt
1 large pinch powdered saffron
3 tbsp. heavy cream
freshly ground black pepper
⅓ cup freshly grated Parmesan
cheese

Preparation time: 40 minutes

710 cal. per serving

1 Boil the meat broth with the marrow bone for about 5 minutes. Peel and finely chop the onion. Melt half the butter in a heavy saucepan and sauté the onion over a low heat until soft and lightly browned.

2 Add the rice to the onion and stir until the grains become transparent. Add the wine and cook until the wine is absorbed. Add the hot broth a little at a time and cook, uncovered, over medium heat, for 10 minutes, stirring frequently. Season with salt.

3 Dissolve the saffron in 3 tbsp. of broth and add to the rice. Remove the marrow from the bone, crush with a spoon, and stir into the rice. Continue to cook over medium heat for a further 5 minutes, stirring constantly, and adding more broth if necessary. The rice should be tender but still firm.

4 Stir the cream and the remaining butter into the cooked rice. Season with pepper and serve at once, accompanied by the grated Parmesan.

Wine: A young, red wine, such as a Barbera from the Piedmont region, goes well with this dish.

Rice

Rice cultivation first spread to southern Europe from India and the Orient in medieval times, but was not firmly established in Italy until the 16th century. By the 19th century, the grain – at one time prescribed as a "light diet" for the sick – became the favorite food of the upper classes and was the cause of a dramatic upturn in the local economies of Turin and Milan. Today, Italy is Europe's leading producer of rice, most of it grown on the humid, alluvial plains of the Po Valley, in Lombardy and Piedmont, including areas around Novara and Vercelli (above, right).

Rice plants like water and warmth. In spring in the Po Valley,

young seedlings are transplanted from seed-beds to artificially flooded paddy-fields and remain partially submerged throughout the growing season. In summer, the crop is harvested, dried, threshed, and processed.

Italian medium and round-grained rice is classified as *commune*,

semifino, and *fino*. Of the latter, arborio and vialone make the best risotto, the most popular way to cook rice in northern Italy. Because of their high starch content, the grains swell to about three times their original size during cooking, yet remain firm.

Ravioli al burro

Buttered Ravioli Stuffed with Spinach

Serves 4 to 6

For the dough:
3 ½ cups all-purpose flour
4 eggs
salt
1 tbsp. olive oil
For the filling:
4 cups fresh spinach
1 small bunch flat-leafed parsley
(about 1 oz.)
1 egg
1 ¼ cups ricotta cheese
⅔ cup freshley grated Parmesan
cheese
salt
grated nutmeg
freshly ground black pepper
For serving:
7 tbsp. butter
8 fresh sage leaves
4 tbsp. freshly grated Parmesan
cheese
freshly ground pepper

Preparation time: 2 hours

**690 cal. per serving
(if serving 6)**

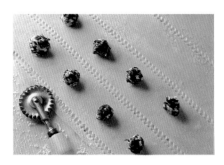

1 On a flat surface, such as a pastry board, form a mound of the all-purpose flour. Make a well in the center, break in the eggs (or whisk in a bowl and then pour them in), and add a pinch of salt. Gradually incorporate the surrounding flour and, work it into a dough with the addition of a little water. Blend in the oil to make the dough more elastic. Knead vigorously by hand. Shape the dough into a ball, cover with a floured cloth, and leave to stand for about 15 minutes.

2 Meanwhile, make the filling. Trim and wash the spinach. Bring a pan of salted water to the boil and cook the spinach over high heat for about 3 minutes. Drain, rinse in cold water, squeeze dry, and chop finely. Wash the parsley, shake dry, and chop finely. Whisk the egg in a mixing bowl. Add the spinach, parsley, ricotta, and Parmesan. Season with salt, nutmeg, and pepper. Mix thoroughly.

3 Divide the ball of dough in two and, on a lightly floured surface, roll out each half into a very thin sheet. Using a pastry wheel, cut the pasta into strips 2 inches wide.

4 With the aid of two teaspoons, put hazelnut-size balls of filling on half the strips at 2-inch intervals (above, left).

5 Moisten the spaces between the fillings with water, and lay the remaining strips of dough on top. With your fingertips, press gently to seal each filling (above, right), then cut into squares. Spread the ravioli on a floured cloth and leave to dry a little.

6 In a large saucepan, bring 3 quarts salted water to the boil. Add the ravioli a few at a time, return the water to the boil, then simmer for 3 to 5 minutes. With a slotted spoon, remove the ravioli from the water, drain them, and arrange on a warmed serving platter.

7 Melt the butter in a small pan with 4 of the sage leaves. Pour the melted butter over the ravioli, sprinkle with the grated Parmesan, and garnish with the remaining sage leaves. Season with pepper. Serve hot.

Wine: Try a light dry white such as Pinot Grigio from Friuli or Orvieto from Umbria.

Lasagne verdi al forno

Complex • Emilia-Romagna

Green lasagne

Serves 4 to 6

For the dough:
1 ¾ cups fresh spinach
2 ½ cups all-purpose flour
3 eggs • salt
2 tbsp. olive oil (optional)

For the meat sauce: see recipe below

For the B chamel sauce:
6 tbsp. butter
2–3 heaping tbsp. all-purpose flour
• 3 cups milk
grated nutmeg • salt

4 tbsp. grated Parmesan cheese
2 tbsp. butter

Preparation time: 2 ½ hours

810 cal. per serving
(if serving 6)

1 Trim and wash the spinach. Put it in a covered pan and steam briefly in the water clinging to the leaves. Squeeze dry and chop very finely.

2 Prepare the dough as described on page 55, Step 1, adding the spinach with the eggs – and, if you wish, the oil – when kneading. Cover with a cloth and leave to stand for 30 minutes.

3 Meanwhile, make the meat sauce according to Steps 1, 2, and 3 below.

4 Prepare the Béchamel sauce. Melt the butter in a saucepan and stir in the all-purpose flour. Gradually add the milk, stirring continuously. Season with nutmeg and salt. Bring to the boil and, using a whisk, continue to cook while beating constantly, until the sauce thickens.

5 Roll the dough out to a thickness of ⅛ inch and cut into rectangles. Bring 3 quarts salted water to the boil, adding a few drops of oil. Cook the rectangles, a few at a time, until they float to the surface. Remove carefully, drain well, and arrange on a damp cloth.

6 Preheat the oven to 350 degrees. Grease an ovenproof dish with a little butter. Arrange a layer of lasagne in the base, cover with a layer of meat sauce, then a thin layer of Béchamel, and sprinkle with Parmesan. Repeat the layers until all ingredients are used up, ending with Parmesan. Dot with flakes of butter. Bake in the oven for about 30 minutes.

Note: Cooked, vacuum-packed, or dried lasagne can also be used in this dish.

Tagliatelle al ragù

Not difficult • Bologna

Tagliatelle with meat sauce

Serves 4

1 large onion • 2 carrots
1 stick celery • ½ oz. parsley
2 oz. prosciutto or ham
2 oz. smoked bacon
4 tbsp. butter
1 ¾ cups ground beef
½ cup red wine • ½ cup meat broth
1 ¼ lb fresh plum tomatoes or
drained canned tomatoes
1 bay leaf • salt and pepper
1 cup milk
14 oz. egg tagliatelle • ¼ tsp. oil
5 tbsp. grated Parmesan cheese

Preparation time: 1 ½ hours

950 cal. per serving

1 Peel and finely chop the onion. Trim, wash, and finely chop the carrots and celery. Wash, dry, and finely chop the parsley. Dice the prosciutto, or ham, and the bacon.

2 Melt the butter in a large saucepan. Add the onion, prosciutto, and bacon, and sauté briefly to soften, stirring constantly. Add the carrots, celery, and parsley and continue to cook for 8 to 10 minutes. Add the ground beef and cook until lightly browned. Pour on the wine, cover, and cook over high heat until the liquid has evaporated. Add the broth and continue to cook and stir to mix the ingredients.

3 If using fresh tomatoes, plunge them in boiling water and skin. Chop the tomatoes and add them to the pan together with the bay leaf. Season with salt and pepper. Cover, and simmer over low heat for about 20 minutes, or until the sauce begins to thicken. Stir in the milk and simmer for a further 10 minutes, or until the milk is absorbed.

4 Bring a large pan of salted water to the boil, add the oil and cook the pasta until it is al dente. Drain and place the tagliatelle in a warmed bowl. Top with the meat sauce and serve immediately, handing the parmesan in a separate bowl.

Tortellini mare-orto

Simple • Emilia-Romagna   **Tortellini with Vegetable and Shrimp Sauce**   *Serves 4*

2 zucchini
3 ½ oz. fresh rocket
salt
⅓ cup freshly shelled, or frozen, peas
4 tbsp. butter
1 cup cooked, shelled shrimp
3 tbsp. grappa
½ cup heavy cream
¼ tsp. oil
2 cups tortellini with mushroom filling
about 1 oz. dill
white pepper

Preparation time: 30 minutes

710 cal. per serving

1 Wash, top, and tail the zucchini and slice them. Finely chop the rocket. Bring a pan of salted water to the boil. If using fresh peas, boil them for 5 to 10 minutes, if using frozen ones cook only until the water comes back to the boil. Add the zucchini and rocket, and cook for a further 2 minutes. Drain thoroughly.

2 Melt the butter in a skillet. Add the peas, zucchini, and rocket. After 5 minutes, add the shrimp and grappa and stir thoroughly. Cover, and cook over medium heat for another 5 minutes, stirring occasionally. Finally, stir in the cream.

3 Bring a pan of salted water to the boil, add the oil, and cook the tortellini until al dente. Meanwhile, wash and finely chop the dill.

4 Drain the tortellini through a colander, put them in a warmed bowl with the vegetable sauce, and mix them together. Season with salt and pepper, sprinkle with dill and serve at once.

Wine: A dry white wine, such as a Verdicchio from the Marches, would be a good choice.

Variation:
Tortellini al prosciutto e panna
(Tortellini with Ham and Cream sace) Cook 52 cups meat-filled tortellini in salted water with a few drops of olive oil and a sage leaf, until al dente. Melt 4 tbsp. butter in a pan. Add ½ cup diced prosciutto or ham and sauté briefly. Stir in 1 cup cream, simmer gently for 5 minutes and season with salt, pepper and a pinch of nutmeg. Mix the well-drained tortellini with the sauce, add 7 tbsp. freshly grated Parmesan cheese and stir thoroughly. Serve hot.

Note: Tortellini can be bought fresh, vacuum-packed, or frozen, with a variety of fillings. Alternatively, the sauce can be served with tagliatelle.

Rocket

Rocket or arugula, *ruca* or *rucola* in Italian, is a salad vegetable widely cultivated around the Mediterranean. In Italy, it is usually sold in the market. Rocket is a fast-growing, aromatic plant, whose dandelion-like leaves have a distinctive, sharp flavor. The plants, are sown in spring and grow to a height of about 30 inches; the first leaves are ready for picking after two months, and they can then be harvested for most of the year.

With the exception of the red-and-white flowers, which bloom from May through July, every part of the rocket plant is edible. Young, tender leaves are used raw in salads. When cooked, the slightly bitter, darker leaves add a spicy tang to rice or pasta dishes (opposite). Puréed with Parmesan and pine nuts, rocket leaves provide an interesting variation on the traditional Genoese pesto (page 64). The roots are especially high in vitamins and minerals, and the oil-rich seeds can be used for seasoning in the same way as mustard seed.

Compared to other salad greens, rocket is relatively expensive, but it grows quickly and is easy to cultivate. Many people grow it from seed in the garden or window box.

Farfalle al Gorgonzola

Quick and easy • Lombardy

Farfalle with Gorgonzola Sauce

Serves 4

salt
¼ tsp. oil
1 sage leaf
14 oz. farfalle (butterfly pasta)
5-7 oz. mild Gorgonzola cheese
5 tbsp. butter
1 cup cream
freshly ground white pepper
4 tbsp. freshly grated Parmesan
cheese

Preparation time: 30 minutes

810 cal. per serving

1 Bring a large pan of salted water to the boil. Add the oil and sage leaf, and cook the pasta until it is al dente.

2 While the pasta is cooking, dice the Gorgonzola. Melt the butter in a large saucepan, add the Gorgonzola, and melt slowly over low heat. Gradually add the cream, stirring constantly. Season with salt and pepper. Continue to cook and stir the sauce for about 5 minutes, until it has thickened to a creamy consistency. If it becomes too thick, add a little pasta water. Stir in 1 to 2 tbsp. of the grated Parmesan.

3 Drain the pasta thoroughly and stir it into the Gorgonzola sauce. Remove the sage leaf. Pour the pasta into a warm bowl and serve at once, handing the remaining Parmesan separately.

Wine: A light red – for example, a Valpolicella from the Verona area – is a good accompaniment.

Note: Though this dish is simple and quick to make, it is delicious and impressive enough to be served to guests.

Rigatoni al sugo di noci

Fairly easy • Liguria

Rigatoni with Walnut Sauce

serves 4

1 ½ cups shelled walnuts
1 tbsp. pine nuts
4 tbsp. butter
1 garlic clove
salt
¼ tsp. oil
1 ¾ cups rigatoni
⅔ cup freshly grated Parmesan
cheese
freshly ground white pepper
about 4 tbsp. basil leaves
virgin olive oil (optional)

Preparation time: 45 minutes

880 cal. per serving

1 Briefly plunge the walnuts into boiling water to loosen the skins, then peel off the skins. Reserve 10 walnut halves for garnish. Using a pestle and mortar or a food processor, grind the rest of the walnuts together with the pine nuts.

2 Melt the butter in a small skillet. Add the ground nuts to the pan and sauté for 4 to 5 minutes, stirring constantly. Peel the garlic clove and soak it in hot water for about 2 minutes to lessen its pungent flavor. Then cut it into very fine slices and stir into the nut mixture.

3 Bring a large pan of salted water to the boil, add the ¼ tsp. oil, and cook the pasta until it is al dente.

4 Pour the nut butter into a warmed serving bowl. Stir in half the Parmesan and a little of the pasta water. Season with salt and pepper.

5 Wash and dry the basil leaves. Drain the pasta through a colander, add it to the bowl and mix thoroughly with the walnut sauce. Garnish with the walnut halves and basil leaves and, if you like, sprinkle with a little olive oil. Serve, handing the remaining Parmesan in a separate bowl.

Note: Walnut sauce is also good with tagliatelle or ravioli. To make the sauce even smoother, you can add about 2 tbsp. light cream.

Pasta con le sarde

Takes time • Sicily

Pasta with Sardines and Fennel

Serves 4

14 oz. fresh sardines
(or other small fish)
salt
1 fennel bulb (about 8 oz.)
1 onion
8 tbsp. virgin olive oil
3 anchovy fillets canned in oil
4 tbsp. pine nuts
4 tbsp yellow raisins
freshly ground pepper
1 large pinch powdered saffron
14 oz. bucatini or macaroni

Preparation time: 1 ½ hours

830 cal. per serving

1 Gut and bone the sardines. Cut off the heads and discard. Wash in salted water and dry.

2 Wash and trim the fennel, reserving a few leaves for garnish. Bring 2 quarts salted water to the boil, and cook the fennel for 10 to 15 minutes. Drain, reserving the cooking water, and cut into small pieces.

3 Peel and finely chop the onion. Heat 5 tbsp. of the olive oil in a skillet and sauté the onion until transparent. Add the drained anchovy fillets and half the sardines, crushing them with a wooden spoon. Add the fennel, pine nuts, and yellow raisins. Season with salt, pepper, and saffron. Add a little fennel water to moisten the mixture and simmer for about 15 minutes.

4 Preheat the oven to 400 degrees. Bring a large pan of salted water to the boil, add a few drops of oil, and cook the pasta until al dente.

5 In a skillet, heat the remaining oil and fry the reserved sardines for 2 minutes on either side. Season with salt and pepper. Drain the pasta and put alternate layers of pasta and sauce in an ovenproof dish. Top with the fried sardines. Cover and bake in the oven for 10 to 15 minutes. Serve, garnished with the reserved fennel leaves.

Penne all'arrabbiata

Not difficult • Lazio

Penne with Chili Sauce

Serves 4

3 ½ oz. smoked fat bacon
2 cups button mushrooms, or porcini wild mushrooms
2 cups ripe or canned tomatoes
2 garlic cloves
salt
¼ tsp. oil
14 oz. penne
4 tbsp. butter
2 small dried chili peppers
6 to 8 basil leaves
4 tbsp. freshly grated pecorino cheese

Preparation time: 45 minutes

670 cal. per serving

1 Cut the bacon into short, thin strips. Trim, rinse, and slice the mushrooms. If using fresh tomatoes, skin and deseed them (page 41, Step 3) or drain canned tomatoes. Dice the tomato flesh. Peel and finely slice the garlic.

2 Bring a large pan of salted water to the boil, add the oil, and cook the pasta until it is al dente.

3 Meanwhile, melt the butter in a large sauté pan, add the bacon and garlic, and brown lightly. Add the mushrooms and, stirring constantly, sauté 5 to 6 minutes. Add the tomatoes and whole chilies. Season with salt, cover, and cook over medium heat for 15 minutes, adding a little pasta water to moisten the mixture.

4 Drain the penne thoroughly and add them to the pan. Mix the pasta and sauce together. the chili peppers can be removed at this stage. Wash and dry the basil leaves, and use them to garnish the penne. Serve straight from the pan, accompanied by the grated pecorino in a separate bowl.

Note: The spiciness of the sauce is determined by the type of chilies used.

Linguine al pesto genovese

Not difficult • Genoa   **Ribbon Pasta with Pesto**   *Serves 4*

2 garlic cloves
salt
1 large bunch basil
(about 3 ½ oz.)
1 chili pepper (optional • see
Glossary)
1 tbsp. pine nuts
2 tbsp. each freshly grated
Parmesan and pecorino cheese
7 tbsp. virgin olive oil
2 small new potatoes
14 oz. linguine or other narrow
ribbon pasta

Preparation time: 30 minutes

670 cal. per serving

1 Peel the garlic, chop coarsely, put it in a pestle and mortar with a little salt, and grind it well.

2 Wash the basil and shake it dry. Remove the stems and coarsely chop the leaves. If using the chili pepper, halve it lengthwise, remove the seeds, and cut into thin strips. Add the pine nuts, basil, and chili to the mortar and pound everything to a paste.

3 Still using the pestle, stir in the Parmesan and pecorino. If your mortar is small, you can transfer the mixture to a larger bowl at this stage. Very gradually, add the olive oil and continue to stir until the pesto has a creamy consistency.

4 Peel the potatoes, cut them into pieces, and boil in a large saucepan of salted water for about 10 minutes. Add the pasta to the pan and cook until it is al dente.

5 Strain the potatoes and pasta through a colander and put them in a warmed bowl. Add the pesto and mix quickly but thoroughly. Serve immediately.

Wine: Serve with a light, dry white wine, such as Vermentino from Liguria.

Note: A less authentic, but quicker, method for making pesto is to put all the ingredients in a food processor or blender and grind them together into a creamy paste.

Basil

Basil was brought to Egypt from India 4,000 years ago and from there found its way to Rome and the rest of southern Europe. It is an essential ingredient in Italian cuisine and is considered by many cooks to be the "queen of herbs." In addition to its culinary reputation, basil – the name comes from the Greek *vasilikos*, meaning "royal" – has long been credited with healing powers. It is said to be a tonic and a tranquilizer, a cure for cramp and a stimulation for jaded appetites.

Basil, essentially a warmth-loving summer plant, can often be seen growing in giant pots on steps or terraces outside Italian houses. The sweetish, peppery taste of sweet basil, the variety usually used for cooking, adds a wonderful flavor to a tomato sauce, meat dishes, or soups, and is the basis of the classic Ligurian pesto (see opposite). The best time for picking is just before or during flowering. It is then that the plant is richest in its aromatic, heady oil. Dried basil is a poor substitute. Italians prefer to preserve the leaves by storing them in layers in a jar, covered in oil. Alternatively, basil can be frozen (though the leaves go dark) and can also be grown successfully on a window sill.

Spaghetti al tonno

Quick and easy • Sicily **Spaghetti with Tuna Sauce** *Serves 4*

⅔ **cup tuna canned in oil**
4 anchovy fillets canned in oil
1 small bunch flat-leafed parsley
(about 1 oz.)
2 garlic cloves
1¾ **cups ripe or canned tomatoes**
3 tbsp. olive oil
1 fresh chili pepper
salt
14 oz. spaghetti
2 tbsp. capers
4 to 6 basil leaves

Preparation time: 30 minutes

550 cal. per serving

1 Drain the tuna and flake it with a fork. Rinse the anchovies under running water and pat dry. Wash the parsley, shake dry, and chop finely. Peel and thinly slice the garlic. If using fresh tomatoes, skin and deseed them (page 41, Step 3). Drain canned tomatoes, if using. Chop the tomatoes.

2 Heat the oil in a heavy saucepan. Add the garlic and whole chili pepper and sauté briefly. Crush the anchovy fillets with a fork, add to the pan, and stir. Add the tomatoes and chopped parsley. Season with a little salt, cover the pan, and simmer over medium heat for 10 to 15 minutes.

3 Meanwhile, bring a large saucepan of salted water to the boil. Add a few drops of oil and cook the pasta until it is al dente.

4 While the pasta is cooking, stir the flaked tuna, and capers into the sauce. Dilute the sauce with a little pasta water, cover, and simmer for about 5 minutes to let the sauce thicken slightly. Remove the chili pepper.

5 Drain the spaghetti in a colander and stir it into the hot sauce. Transfer to a warmed serving bowl. Garnish with the basil leaves and, of you like, drizzle a little olive oil over the top before serving.

Spaghetti alla carbonara

Quick and easy • Lazio **Spaghetti with Bacon and Eggs** *Serves 4*

6 oz. rindless pancetta
or slab bacon
1 tbsp. olive oil
2 tbsp. butter
14 oz. spaghetti
4 egg yolks
2 tbsp. sour cream
7 tbsp. freshly grated Parmesan
cheese
salt
freshly ground black pepper
freshly grated nutmeg

Preparation time: 30 minutes

790 cal. per serving

1 Cut the bacon into small dice. Heat the oil and butter in a heavy saucepan. Fry the bacon over a low heat until the fat runs out.

2 Bring a large pan of salted water to the boil, add a few drops of oil, and cook the spaghetti until it is al dente.

3 Meanwhile, put the egg yolks in a bowl and beat them until frothy. Stir in the sour cream and half the Parmesan. Season with salt, pepper, and grated nutmeg.

4 Drain the spaghetti in a colander and add to the bacon in the pan. Stir

together briefly, then remove the pan from the heat. Quickly stir the egg mixture into the spaghetti, season with pepper, and serve immediately. Pass the remaining grated Parmesan in a separate bowl.

Note: This is a classic dish, but there are also many variations. The sour cream can be omitted, or replaced by warmed, fresh heavy cream. Minced onions can be added to the bacon. To ensure that the eggs do not form lumps and the sauce stays creamy, the egg mixture must be incorporated very fast, and away from the heat. A little more cream can be added if necessary.

Gnocchi de patate

Potato Gnocchi with Ricotta

2 ¼ *lb. floury potatoes*
salt
1 egg plus 1 egg yolk
about 1 ⅓ cups all-purpose flour
7 oz. smoked or unsmoked ricotta
⅔ cup butter
6 to 8 sage leaves
freshly grated nutmeg
freshly ground black pepper
4 tbsp. freshly grated Parmesan cheese

Preparation time: 2 hours

790 cal. per serving

1 Boil the potatoes in salted water until tender. Drain and peel. Mash them thoroughly or purée them through a metal sieve. Leave to cool.

2 Add the egg, egg yolk and a little salt to the puréed potatoes and knead together on a pastry board, using enough of the flour to make a smooth, workable dough. Make sure hands and board are well-floured. The dough should not stick to the fingers.

3 Divide the dough into fist-size portions. Use floured hands to shape each serving into a cylinder about the thickness of a finger. Cut each dough cylinder into pieces about 1 inch long (*above*) and sprinkle each piece with a little flour.

4 Bring a large saucepan of salted water to the boil. Slip the gnocchi into the water a few at a time. Cover the pan and cook over low heat for 3 to 5 minutes. The gnocchi should float to the surface when they are done.

5 Meanwhile, cut the ricotta into small, thin slices. Melt half the butter in a large skillet and gently brown 4 of the sage leaves. Add the ricotta to the pan (below, left) and move it about in the butter.

6 Remove the gnocchi from the pan with a slotted spoon. Drain thoroughly and transfer to the pan. Add the remaining butter and stir to mix the ricotta and gnocchi. Season with nutmeg and pepper. Serve straight from the pan or in a warmed bowl, garnished with sage leaves and accompanied by the grated Parmesan.

Wine: A dry red wine with character, such as Teroldego Rotaliano from Trentino, goes well with gnocchi.

Variation:
Gnocchi verdi (Spinach gnocchi) Cook and mash 2 ¼ lb. potatoes. Finely chop 2 cups fresh, or ½ cup thawed, frozen spinach. Squeeze out as much moisture as possible and mix with the mashed potatoes, 1 ⅓ cups flour, and 1 egg yolk. Prepare the gnocchi as shown above, pour 1 ⅓ cups melted butter over them and sprinkle with grated Parmesan.

Note: To make firmer gnocchi, add a little more flour to the dough. Smoked ricotta is a delicious souvenir to bring back from northern Italy; it keeps well if wrapped and stored in the refrigerator.

Polenta con tartufi

Polenta with Cheese and White Truffles

1 ¼ cups cornmeal (see Glossary)
salt
7 oz. fontina cheese
7 tbsp. butter
1 ⅓ cups freshly grated Parmesan
cheese
freshly grond white pepper
1 small piece white truffle
(1- 2 oz.)

Preparation time: 1 hour

710 cal. per serving

1 In a deep, heavy saucepan, bring 5 cups water to the boil and add 1 tbsp. salt. Pour the cornmeal slowly into the boiling water, continuously stirring with a wooden spoon, so that it does not form lumps. Lower the heat and simmer for about 30 minutes, stirring constantly, until the polenta thickens, adding more water if necessary.

2 Dice the fontina and stir it into the polenta. In a small pan, heat the butter until it foams. Stir 60 g of the Parmesan and the melted butter into the polenta. Cook for another 5 minutes, stirring vigorously. For this recipe the polenta should be quite soft and creamy. Season with pepper, and more salt if required.

3 Cut the raw truffle into very thin slices, using a sharp knife or potato peeler – or, if you have one, a truffle slicer. Using a ladle, transfer the polenta to a warmed serving dish and sprinkle with the remaining Parmesan. Top with the truffle slices.

Variation:
Polenta al piatto con ragù
(Polenta with meat sauce)
Make a meat sauce following the recipe on page 57. Using only cornmeal and water, prepare a polenta as in Step 1, above. Serve with the sauce, on individual plates, accompanied by grated Parmesan.

Polenta fritta

Fried polenta

300 g cornmeal (see Glossary)
salt
olive oil or butter
freshly ground black pepper
100 g freshly grated Parmesan
cheese (optional)

Preparation time: 1 hour
(plus 2 hours for cooling)

810 cal. per serving

1 Using only water and cornmeal, make firm polenta following Step 1 in the recipe on the opposite page.

2 Turn out the hot polenta onto a flat surface or large wooden board. Spread it out to make a smooth rectangle about 2 inches thick and leave to cool for about 2 hours. Using fine string, cut it into slices ½ inch wide.

3 Heat the olive oil or butter in a large skillet. Fry the polenta slices both sides, until they are crisp and golden-brown.

4 Drain the slices on kitchen paper, season with pepper, and arrange on a warmed serving dish. If you like, sprinkle them with Parmesan cheese.

Variation:

Frittelle di polenta alla lodigiana

(Polenta Rissoles with Fontina)
Make polenta as in Step 1 (opposite page) using 6 cups milk instead of the water. Unmold onto a flat surface, spread into a smooth ½ inch layer, and leave to cool. Press the rim of a glass in all-purpose flour and cut out 30 circles. Place a slice of fontina cheese on half of them, cover with the other circles and press gently together. Whisk 2 eggs in a deep bowl with a little salt. Dip the rissoles in the beaten egg, one by one, and roll in bread crumbs. Heat 5 tbsp. olive oil in a skillet. Fry the rissoles on both sides until crisp.

SECONDI PIATTI: PESCE

A long the Italian coasts, fish and other seafood still take pride of place as the entrée in traditional menus. Although many types of fish which were once abundant have disappeared from the Mediterranean, and the number of fish caught has diminished considerably in recent years, Italy still has plenty of fresh and saltwater fish and a wealth of shellfish to choose from. These provide the basis for delicious inventions. Among the best known – popular in every region – is *fritto misto di mare*, a medley of small fish and seafood, floured and crisply fried. Mussels, clams, and squid appear in all sorts of appealing dishes. Humbler fish have inspired one of the most famous dishes, *Cacciucco alla livornese*, a mouth-watering stew originally made from scraps by poor fisher folk and now found in dozens of variations. The *Cacciucco alla viareggina* overleaf is from the Tuscan coast.

Care and imagination are the characteristics of Mediterranean fish and shellfish cookery. The result is that whether broiled or fried, steamed or stuffed, encased in pastry or baked on a bed of vegetables, these dishes have one thing in common – they all taste great.

Cacciucco alla viareggina

Complex • Viareggio **Mixed Fish Stew** *Serves 6*

1 lb. 5 oz. mixed, medium-to-small
fish (for example, mackerel, porgy,
grouper)
1 lb. two oz. assorted fish fillets (for
example, sea bream, cod, gray
mullet, sea bass, monkfish, sole)
10 ½ oz. cleaned, small squid
2 cups mussels
10 ½ oz. fresh shrimp
1 onion
1 carrot
2 sticks celery
6 garlic cloves
salt
1 lb. 5 oz. fresh, ripe tomatoes, or
canned tomatoes
6 tbsp. virgin olive oil
2 dried chili peppers
1 cup dry white wine
1 large pinch powdered saffron
(optional)
1 small bunch parsley (about 1 oz.)
6 or 12 slices crusty white bread

Preparation time: 1 ½ hours

450 cal. per serving

1 Gut and scale the small fish, and wash thoroughly under running water. Cut off the heads and fins (*above*). Cut the fish fillets into 1-inch pieces. Trim and rinse the squid and cut into rings about ½ inch wide. Wash, scrape, and beard the mussels (page 36, Step 3); tap sharply any that are open and discard if they don't close. Wash and shell the shrimp and remove the dark vein-like intestines.

2 Peel and coarsely chop the onion and carrot. Trim, wash, string, and chop the celery. Peel the garlic. Put the whole fish in a pan containing 1 quart salted water and bring to the boil. Add the chopped vegetables and 2 garlic cloves and simmer over low heat for about 30 minutes.

3 Meanwhile, bring 1 cup water to the boil in another saucepan. Add the mussels, cover, and cook for about 5 minutes over high heat, or until the shells open. Discard any unopened mussels. Strain the mussel broth through a fine sieve and add to the fish and vegetable broth. Reserve 8 mussels in their shells for garnish and remove the rest from their shells.

4 Plunge fresh tomatoes in boiling water and skin them, or drain canned tomatoes. Chop the tomato flesh. Heat

5 tbsp. of the olive oil in a large, heavy pan. Add 3 whole garlic cloves, the squid, and the whole chilies and sauté briefly. Add the chopped tomatoes and cook, stirring, until the sauce thickens, then stir in the wine. Cover the pan and simmer for 15 minutes. Season with salt and the saffron, if desired.

5 Remove the whole fish from the broth and separate the flesh from the bones. Strain the broth through a sieve into another pan and discard the vegetables. Rub the fish flesh through the sieve and put it back into the broth.

6 Place the firmer-fleshed fish fillets in the tomato sauce in the heavy pan. Add half the fish broth and simmer gently for about 5 minutes. Add the more delicately fleshed fish fillets (e.g. sole and monkfish), the shelled mussels and shrimp, and pour in the remaining broth. Simmer for a further 2 minutes. Remove and discard the garlic cloves and chilies. Wash, dry, and mince the parsley, sprinkle it over the stew, and garnish with the reserved mussels.

7 Toast the slices of bread. Rub them with the remaining garlic clove and sprinkle with the rest of the oil. Serve the stew, in soup plates, accompanied by the toast.

Wine: A dry white wine, such as a Vernaccia di San Gimignano from Tuscany, is a good choice – or perhaps a Verdicchio from the Marches.

Variation: Put the slices of toasted bread, rubbed with garlic and sprinkled with oil, in the soup plates and pour the fish stew over them.

Triglie alla Livornese

Not difficult • Livorno

Red mullet in Spicy Tomato Sauce

Serves 4

1 stick celery
1 small bunch parsley
(about 1 oz.)
3 cups ripe tomatoes
3 garlic cloves
5 tbsp. virgin olive oil
1 dried chili pepper
salt
½ cup dry red wine
8 small or 4 large red mullet
(about 2 lb. 10 oz. in weight)

Preparation time: 1 hour

500 cal. per serving

1 Trim, wash, and string the celery, and cut it into ½ inch pieces. Wash the parsley, shake dry, and chop finely. Skin and deseed the tomatoes (page 41, Step 3). Chop them into small pieces. Peel and thinly slice the garlic.

2 Heat the olive oil in a large sauté pan. Add the garlic and half the parsley, and sauté briefly. Add the vegetables and the chili pepper. Stir and season with salt. Cover the pan and simmer over medium heat for about 20 minutes. From time to time, add a little of the red wine.

3 Meanwhile, gut and scale the red mullet and wash it under running water. Soak the fish in cold, salted water for about 15 minutes, and dry thoroughly.

4 Place the fish carefully in the pan with the sauce. Cover, and simmer over low heat for 15 to 20 minutes, without turning the fish. Transfer the fish and sauce to a warmed dish, sprinkle with the remaining parsley, and serve accompanied by slices of crusty white bread.

Calamari ripieni

Slightly more complex • Sardinia

Stuffed Squid

Serves 4

8 medium-sized squid (2 ¼ lb.)
juice of half a lemon
4 anchovy fillets in oil
1 small bunch parsley (about 1 oz.)
1 sprig rosemary
2 garlic cloves
1 egg
3 tbsp. bread crumbs
salt
freshly ground black pepper
3 tbsp. olive oil
¾ cup dry white wine
6 tbsp. sieved tomatoes

Preparation time: 1 ½ hours

430 cal. per serving

1 Clean the medium-sized squid (page 36, Step 1), discarding the ink sacs. Sprinkle the inside of the body pouches with the lemon juice. Chop the squid tentacles into small pieces.

2 Rinse, pat dry, and finely chop the anchovy fillets. Wash, dry, and finely chop the parsley and rosemary. Peel and finely chop the garlic. In a bowl, whisk the egg, then stir in the herbs, chopped anchovies, squid tentacles, and bread crumbs. Season with a little salt and pepper.

3 Fill the body pouches loosely with the mixture, and sew up with white thread. Heat the oil in a large, heavy pan. Brown the squid on all sides over high heat. Sprinkle with a few extra

drops of oil and pour in the wine. Cover, and braise over low heat for about 25 minutes, or until tender (test by pricking with a fork). Add the sieved tomatoes, season with salt and pepper, and cook for another 5 minutes.

Wine: Serve a dry white wine, or try a light-bodied young red wine, such as a Merlot from Veneto.

Variation:
(Stuffed squid with Swiss chard)
Cut the green leaves of 1 lb. 2 oz. Swiss chard into ½ inch strips, blanch in boiling salted water, rinse in cold water, and squeeze dry. Add to the squid instead of the tomatoes (Step 4, above) and cook for 5 minutes.

Cozze gratinate alla tarantina

Simple • Taranto

Mussels au Gratin

Serves 4

4'₂ lb. fresh mussels
1 large bunch flat-leafed parsley
(about 2 oz.)
4 garlic cloves
6 tbsp. bread crumbs
6 tbsp. freshly grated pecorino
cheese
10 tbsp. virgin olive oil
salt
freshly ground black pepper
2 lemons

Preparation time: 1 hour

550 cal. per serving

1 Scrape, wash, and beard the mussels (page 36, Step 3). Tap sharply any shells that are open, and discard any that don't close. Bring 2 quarts of water to a boil, add the mussels, cover the pan and cook over high heat until the mussels open. Discard any mussels that remain closed.

2 Wash, shake dry and finely chop the parsley. Peel and finely chop the garlic. Put the parsley and garlic in a bowl together with the bread crumbs, pecorino cheese, and 7 tbsp. of the oil. Season with salt and pepper, and mix thoroughly.

3 Preheat the oven to 400 degrees. Split the cooled mussels and discard the empty half-shells. Spread the mussel halves with the bread crumb mixture and arrange in a shallow ovenproof dish. Bake for about 10 minutes, until lightly browned.

4 Wash the lemons and cut each one into eight wedges. Sprinkle the mussels with the remaining olive oil and garnish with the lemon wedges. Serve with crusty white bread.

Wine: An Apulian rosé, such as Castel del Monte, goes well with mussels.

Shellfish

While mussels are favorites in Italian cooking, other bivalves, including clams, scallops, cockles, razor-clams, and of course oysters, are popular too. Nowadays, mussels are mostly cultivated. In Italy's mussel beds, these blue-black shellfish are usually grown vertically, clinging via secreted, byssal threads to ropes made of grass or hemp. When the mussels reach marketable size – between 2 and 4 inches long – the ropes are hauled onto boats and the shellfish are harvested. Like mussels (*cozze*, or the Adriatic *peoci*), clams (*vongole*) often appear on the menu in pasta or risotto dishes, or a part

of a seafood stew or salad. Clams, with their characteristic grooved spiral stripes, are available in many sizes and colors. Razor-clams from the bay of La Spezia are a particular delicacy. Scallops are found along the Adriatic coast, and heart-shaped cockles live in muddy of sandy areas to a depth of

about 40 feet. Specially equipped boats are used to harvest clams and cockles. High-pressure pumps drive water into the seabed and the swirling sand is sucked up together with the shellfish through a pipe onto the boat.

78 *Secondi piatti: pesce*

Fritto misto del golfo

Mixed fried fish

Not difficult · Campania

Serves 4

1 lb. 2 oz. small fish (for example,
fresh anchovies, whitebait, tiny sole)
10½ oz. cleaned small squid, or
cuttlefish
10½ oz. fresh shrimp
all-purpose flour for coating
vegetable oil for frying
3 lemons
salt

Preparation time: 1 hour

240 cal. per serving

1 Thoroughly clean the fish. Remove the heads, fins, and scales and rinse under running water. Put the fish to soak in a bowl of cold, salted water for about 15 minutes.

2 Meanwhile, wash the squid or cuttlefish. Cut the pouches into rings and, if large, the tentacles into smaller pieces. Shell the shrimp, leaving the tail ends on. Remove the dark, vein-like intestines.

3 Drain the fish and pat dry, then coat them in all-purpose flour. Heat a generous amount of vegetable oil in a deep skillet and fry the coated fish, a few at a time, until crisp on both sides,

reducing the heat after a minute or so to ensure that they also cook on the inside. Remove with a slotted spoon, drain on kitchen paper and keep hot in a low oven. In the same way, fry the squid, or cuttlefish, and the shrimp until golden-brown.

4 Wash the lemons in hot water, wipe dry and cut into wedges. Arrange all the seafood on a warmed serving dish, garnish with the lemon, sprinkle with a little salt and serve very hot.

Wine: A well-chilled, dry white wine, such as a Sauvignon from Friuli, is good with Fritto misto.

Gamberoni allo spiedo

Skewered Shrimp with Caper Sauce

Simple · Liguria

Serves 4

2 garlic cloves
1 small bunch flat-leafed parsley
(about 1 oz.)
10 tbsp. virgin olive oil
32 raw or cooked jumbo shrimp
(about 1 lb. 12 oz.)
salt and freshly ground black
pepper · 1 tbsp. capers
2 anchovy fillets canned in oil
3 pitted black olives
1 tbsp. pine nuts
2 lemons · 1 egg yolk

*Preparation time: about 1½ hours
(including marinating time)*

480 cal. per serving

1 Peel and finely chop the garlic. Wash and dry the parsley, and chop half of it. Put the garlic and chopped parsley in a soup plate and mix together with half the oil.

2 Wash and dry the shrimp, season them with salt and pepper, and place in the marinade. Marinate for about 1 hour, turning them from time to time.

3 Meanwhile, prepare the sauce. Drain the capers and anchovy fillets and purée them in a food processor with the olives, pine nuts, the rest of the parsley, and the juice of half a lemon. Beat the egg yolk in a bowl until frothy. Gradually stir

in the remaining oil. Finally, add the purée and stir to make a smooth sauce. Season with salt and pepper.

4 Preheat the broiler. Thread the shrimp onto 8 skewers, 4 to each skewer. Broil raw shrimp for about 10 minutes on each side, or 2 minutes for cooked shrimp, brushing with a little oil.

5 Serve on warmed plates, garnished with lemon wedges and accompanied by the sauce and crusty bread.

Note: Skewered shrimp taste even better when broiled over a charcoal grill.

Torta di pesce

Fish and Vegetable Flan

For the pastry:
½ cup butter
2 cups all-purpose flour
½ tsp. salt
about 4 tbsp. milk

For the filling:
1 lb. 2 oz. fish fillets
(for example, cod, red snapper, or sea bass)
juice of 1 lemon
¾ cup round-grain rice
salt
1 pinch powdered saffron (optional)
2 eggs
¾ cup freshly grated Parmesan cheese
freshly ground white pepper
2 small onions
1 carrot
1 stick celery
1 small bunch flat-leafed parsley (1 oz.)
1½ cups button mushrooms
4 tbsp. olive oil
⅔ cup freshly shelled, or frozen, peas
½ cup white wine
1 garlic clove
2 tbsp. raisins
2 tbsp. pine nuts
3 tbsp. butter
1 tbsp. bread crumbs

Preparation time: 2 hours
(Plus 1 hour standing and
30 minutes to marinate)

760 cal. per serving
(if serving 6)

1 Cut the butter into pieces. Put the all-purpose flour in a bowl with the salt, add the butter, and rub it in. Knead with enough cold milk to make a smooth dough. Cover and refrigerate for about 1 hour.

2 Rinse the fish and pat it dry. Sprinkle with the lemon juice and marinate for about 30 minutes.

3 Cook the rice in 2 cups boiling salted water, until the liquid is absorbed. If using, dissolve the saffron in 3 tbsp. hot water and stir into the rice. Whisk the eggs and stir into the rice with 4 tbsp. of the grated Parmesan. Season with pepper. Leave to cool.

4 Peel the onions and carrot, wash and string the celery, wash and dry the parsley, and finely chop them all. Trim

the mushrooms, rinse briefly under running water, pat dry and slice.

5 Heat half the olive oil in a skillet, add the onions, and fry them until transparent. Add the chopped carrot and celery, sauté for a few minutes, then add half the parsley, the sliced mushrooms, and finally the peas. Pour in the white wine and cook over medium heat for 10 to 15 minutes, stirring frequently (*above*). Season with salt.

6 Peel the garlic clove and cut it into thin slices. Sprinkle the fish fillets with salt. Heat the remaining oil in a skillet, add the garlic, and sauté briefly. Add the fish, lightly brown it on both sides, then flake with a fork. Mix in the remaining parsley, raisins, pine nuts and the cooked vegetables. Preheat the oven to 400 degrees.

7 Grease a large flan dish, about 10 inches in diameter, with half the butter

and sprinkle it with the bread crumbs. On a flat surface, roll the dough into a circle and lay it in the dish, pulling it up the sides to make a rim. Place half the rice in the pastry case, followed by the fish-and-vegetable mixture, and top with the remaining rice (*above*). Dot the top with the remaining butter cut into flakes. Sprinkle with the rest of the Parmesan and bake in the oven for about 30 minutes, reducing the heat to 350 degrees. Serve the flan either warm or cold, accompanied by a mixed salad.

Wine: Choose an aromatic white wine from the Veneto, such as a Bianco di Custoza.

Orata al forno con patate

Simple • Apulia   **Baked Bream with Potatoes**   *Serves 4*

1 gilthead bream, or sea bream
(about 2 ¼ lb.)
salt
5 medium-sized potatoes
2 garlic cloves
freshly ground black pepper
2 sprigs rosemary
6 tbsp. virgin olive oil
6 sage leaves
4 tbsp. dry white wine
1 lemon

Preparation time: 1 ½ hours

480 cal. per serving

1 Gut and scale the fish, and rinse thoroughly inside and out under running water. Soak for about 15 minutes in cold salted water. Meanwhile, peel the potatoes and cut into pieces. Peel the garlic.

2 Pat the fish dry on kitchen paper. Season it inside and out with salt and pepper. Put the whole garlic cloves and one rosemary sprig inside the fish.

3 Preheat the oven to 400 degrees. Pour 3 tbsp. olive oil into a large baking dish. Arrange the potatoes in the bottom of the dish. Sprinkle with the sage leaves and the other rosemary sprig, and top with 1 tbsp. of the olive oil.

Season with salt and pepper and bake in the middle of the oven for about 15 minutes.

4 Lay the fish on the bed of potatoes and bake in the oven for a further 30 to 35 minutes. Baste occasionally with some of the white wine.

5 Cut the lemon into quarters. Sprinkle the fish with the remaining olive oil and serve hot, dividing into portions at the table and garnishing with the lemon.

Wine: A well-chilled Soave Classico, or similar dry white wine, goes well with this fish.

Trota in padella

Fairly easy • Piedmont

Pan-fried Trout

4 fresh trout (9 –10 oz. each)
salt • freshly ground black pepper
2 tbsp. yellow raisins
1 onion • 1 garlic clove
1 stick celery
8 sage leaves
1 sprig rosemary
3 bay leaves
4 tbsp. butter
3 tbsp. white wine vinegar
grated rind of 1 lemon
1¼ cups fish broth
1 tbsp. all-purpose flour

Preparation time: 50 minutes

**400 cal.
per serving**

1 Clean and gut the trout, wash them thoroughly, and pat dry. Season them inside and out with salt and pepper. Soak the yellow raisins in lukewarm water for about 15 minutes.

2 Peel and finely chop the onion and garlic. Trim, wash, string, and finely chop the celery. Rinse the herbs under running water and pat dry.

3 Preheat the oven to 275 degrees. Melt half of the butter in a large skillet and sauté the onion, garlic, and celery for 5 minutes. Add the sage leaves. Place the trout in the pan and fry for 2 to 4 minutes on either side. Add the wine vinegar. Add the grated lemon rind, yellow raisins, rosemary and bay leaves.

Continue to cook, uncovered, for a few minutes over low heat – the fish is ready when the dorsal fins pull off easily. Baste frequently with half the fish broth.

4 Transfer the trout from the skillet to a serving dish and place in the oven to keep warm.

5 Mix the flour with 2 tbsp. water and stir into the liquid in the pan. Bring back to the boil, gradually add the remaining fish broth, and continue to cook for about 5 minutes, or until the sauce thickens. Stir in the remaining butter. Remove the bay leaves and rosemary. Season the sauce with salt and pepper, and serve with the trout.

Sarde ripiene

Needs some care • Sardinia

Stuffed Sardines

Serves 4 to 6

1 bread roll • ½ cup milk
12 large, fresh sardines (about 2 lb.)
salt
juice of half a lemon
4 anchovy fillets canned in oil
1 garlic clove
2 eggs
1 to 2 tbsp. freshly grated pecorino cheese
freshly ground black pepper
all-purpose flour for coating
4 tbsp. olive oil
1 small bunch of parsley (about 1 oz.)
2 lemons for garnish

Preparation time: ½ hours

380 cal. per serving (if serving 6)

1 Cut the bread roll into quarters and soak it in the milk.

2 Meanwhile, scale the sardines and cut off their heads. Slit open along the bellies, gut, and remove the backbones and tails. Wash the fish thoroughly under running water and pat dry. Lightly season the insides with salt and sprinkle with the lemon juice. Preheat the oven to 425 degrees.

3 Squeeze the bread out well and cut into small pieces. Rinse the anchovy fillets and pat dry. Peel the garlic. Using a pestle and mortar, pound the anchovies and garlic to a paste. Add the bread and stir to make a thick creamy mixture. Whisk the eggs in a bowl, add the pecorino to the eggs and stir them into the anchovy paste. Season with salt and pepper.

4 Fill the sardines with the mixture and close the openings by pressing them together. Coat the stuffed fish with a little flour. Pour 3 tbsp. of the olive oil into a baking dish. Arrange the fish in layers and sprinkle with the remaining oil. Bake in the oven for 20 to 30 minutes until golden-brown.

5 Wash the parsley, shake dry, and chop finely. Slice the 2 lemons. Arrange the sardines on a warmed serving dish, sprinkle with parsley, and garnish with halved lemon slices.

Wine: A young Sardinian white wine, such as Nuragus di Cagliari is a good accompaniment.

Tonno fresco in umido

Simple • the Marches

Fresh Tuna Steaks in Tomato Sauce

Serves 4

4 fresh tuna steaks (about 1 lb. 5 oz.)
all-purpose flour for coating
5 tbsp. olive oil
1 small onion
1 stick celery
small bunch flat-leafed parsley (about 1 oz.)
2 cloves • salt
freshly ground black pepper
2 cups sieved tomatoes

Preparation time: 45 minutes

500 cal. per serving

1 Rinse the tuna steaks under running water, dry them, and coat in all-purpose flour. Heat 2 tbsp. of the olive oil in a skillet, add the fish, and briefly cook the steaks on either side. Remove with a slotted spoon and drain on kitchen paper.

2 Peel and finely chop the onion. Trim, wash, string, and finely chop the celery. Wash, dry, and finely chop the parsley. Heat the remaining oil in a skillet. Add the onion and sauté until transparent. Add the celery and half the parsley and continue to cook for about 5 minutes. Add the cloves and season with salt and pepper.

3 Pour the sieved tomatoes over the vegetables and continue to cook for 10 minutes, or until the sauce thickens. Lay the tuna in the sauce and cook, turning occasionally, for another 10 to 20 minutes (depending on the thickness of the slices) until tender.

4 Arrange the tuna steaks on a warmed serving platter. Pour the sauce over the fish and sprinkle with the remaining parsley. Serve hot.

Note: This recipe is also suitable for dentex, sea bream, fresh salmon, or sea bass.

SECONDI PIATTI: CARNE

The Italian golden rule for meat dishes is quality before quantity. Meat is generally eaten in small portions, but is carefully prepared. Beef, veal, pork, lamb, game, and poultry all feature on the menu, often in recipes that reflect the character of the varying regions.

In the north, you will find tender beef or veal pot roasts and stews, or perhaps a dish of boiled meat, such as *Bollito misto*. *Ossobuco*, slices of veal knuckle accompanied by saffron risotto and *gremolata*, a spicy mixture of lemon rind, parsley, and garlic is a specialty of Milan. Other renowned veal dishes include *Saltimbocca alla romana* from Lazio, thin veal scallops fried with ham and sage; and the Piedmontese *Vitello tonnato*, cold braised veal with tuna sauce.

In the Alpine regions, game is served with polenta. In rural areas, squab and guinea fowl are eaten, as well as chickens, which are fed only on corn or wheat grains. The soft-as-butter liver dish called *Fegato alla veneziana* is typically Venetian, while popular dishes in Emilia-Romagna include roast pork and spit-roast suckling pig.

Wild quail is a specialty of the Marches. *Lepre in umido*, braised hare in a spicy sauce is a classic Tuscan dish. The inland farmers of central and southern Italy keep rabbits, sheep, and goats. Traditionally, lamb and kid are slaughtered at Easter and roasted on a spit, baked in the oven, or braised in a stew.

Vitello tonnato

Not difficult • Piedmont   **Cold Veal with Tuna Sauce**   *Serves 6*

1 carrot
1 onion
1 stick celery
2 ¼ lb. boned loin of veal
1 bay leaf
2 cloves
3 cups dry white wine
salt
5 ½ oz. tuna fish canned in oil
3 anchovy fillets canned in oil
2 egg yolks
3 tbsp. capers
2 unwaxed lemons
about ¾ cup olive oil
freshly ground pepper

Preparation time:
2 hours (plus 4 to 5 hours
marinating and chilling time)

670 cal. per serving

1 Peel and coarsely chop the carrot and onion, wash and chop the celery. Put the chopped vegetables in a heatproof casserole together with the veal, bay leaf, cloves, and wine. Cover, and marinate for 24 hours.

2 Add 1 tsp. salt and just enough water to cover the meat. Bring to the boil and simmer over low heat for 1 hour. Leave in the broth until cool.

3 Meanwhile, drain the tuna and the anchovy fillets. Rinse, pat dry, and chop the anchovies. Purée the tuna, anchovies, egg yolks, and 2 tbsp. of the capers with juice of ½ lemon. Gradually stir in a little broth and the olive oil to make a creamy sauce. Season with salt and pepper.

4 Remove the veal from the broth. Cut it into thin slices and arrange on a serving platter. Pour the sauce evenly over the meat. Cover, and refrigerate for 3 to 4 hours. Before serving, thinly slice the remaining 1½ lemons and arrange the slices on top of the meat. Sprinkle with the remaining capers.

Note: This is an elegant summer dish to serve to company.

Capers

Capers are an important flavoring agent in such classic dishes as *Vitello tonnato* (*above*) and *Caponata siciliana* (recipe, page 115). They are the unopened flower buds of the spiny, trailing, pink or white-flowered caper plant, *Capparis spinosa*, which flourishes in arid Mediterranean soil, and is found all over southern Italy, even growing like a weed at the roadside.

The capers used in cooking have little flavor in themselves, although there is some evidence that the Greeks and Romans ate both the flowers and buds. They mostly serve as vehicles for the sharp tastes of pickling ingredients.

The buds range in color from olive to blue-green, and in size from that of a tiny peppercorn to that of a large pea. They are harvested in the early morning, when they are hard and tightly closed. Once collected, the caper buds are left to dry overnight, then sorted by size (*above*) and laid in baths of pure salt, brine, or vinegar, the preservatives that give them flavor.

The preserved capers are graded according to size: the larger they are, the stronger the flavor. The most highly prized are the smallest, most delicately flavored grades known as *nonpareilles* and *capucines*.

Ossobuco alla milanese

Fairly easy • Lombardy **Braised Knuckle of Veal** *Serves 6 to 8*

4 medium-sized carrots
3 medium-sized onions
3 garlic cloves
4 sticks celery
4 tbsp. butter
about 6 ½ lb. knuckle of veal, sawn
through the bone into 6 to 8 slices
salt
freshly ground black pepper
all-purpose flour for coating
6 tbsp. olive oil
1 cup white wine
2 ¼ lb. ripe beefsteak or canned
tomatoes
1 small bunch flat-leafed parsley
(about 1 oz.)
about 2 cups meat broth
½ tsp. fresh thyme
½ tsp. oregano
2 bay leaves

For the gremolata:
1 small bunch flat-leafed parsley
(about 1 oz.)
5 garlic cloves
grated rind of 2 untreated lemons

Preparation time: about 3 hours

570 cal. per serving
(if serving 8)

1 Peel and finely chop the carrots, onions, and garlic. Wash, string, and finely chop the celery. Heat the butter in an ovenproof casserole over low heat. As soon as it has melted, add the vegetables and sauté until lightly browned, stirring constantly (*above*).

2 Tie the slices of meat into neat rounds with kitchen thread (*above*). Season with salt and pepper, and coat with all-purpose flour, shaking to remove any excess. Heat the olive oil in a skillet and fry each slice over medium heat until lightly browned on both sides. As the slices are done, remove them from the pan and arrange them on top of the vegetables in the casserole.

3 Pour off the excess oil and add the wine to the pan juices. Bring to the boil, stirring to dislodge any solid matter, and cook until the liquid reduces to 4 to 6 tablespoons.

4 Preheat the oven to 325 degrees. Briefly plunge fresh tomatoes into boiling water, skin them (*above*), then halve and remove the seeds; or drain canned tomatoes. Cut the tomatoes into pieces. Coarsely chop the parsley, including the stalks.

5 Add 1 cup of the broth to the pan juices, followed by the chopped parsley, thyme, oregano, bay leaves, and tomatoes. Bring to the boil and season with salt and pepper.

6 Pour the sauce over the meat in the casserole. Bring back to the boil, cover, and transfer the casserole to the oven. Cook for 2 to 3 hours, until the meat is tender, adding a little broth every 30 minutes, to replace liquid lost through evaporation.

7 Meanwhile, make the *gremolata*: Wash and finely chop the parsley, peel and finely chop the garlic cloves, and mix them together with the grated lemon rind.

8 Remove the thread from the meat. Place the slices on a serving dish and top with the vegetables and sauce. Finally, sprinkle with the *gremolata*. *Risotto alla milanese* (recipe, page 52) can be served with this dish.

Braciole di maiale alle olive

Pork Chops with Black Olives

4 pork chops
salt
freshly ground pepper
all-purpose flour for coating
6 tbsp. olive oil
1 cup dry white wine
3 ½ oz. Canadian bacon
1 medium-sized onion
1 garlic clove
16 black olives
1 ¼ cups fresh or canned tomatoes
1 small bunch flat-leafed parsley
(about 1 oz.)
1 bay leaf
1 egg

Preparation time: 50 minutes

810 cal. per serving

1 Preheat the oven to 300 degrees. Trim the fat from the chops, making several incisions round the edges so that they do not curl up during frying. Season the chops with salt and pepper and coat with all-purpose flour. Heat half the oil in a sauté pan. Add the chops and, over high heat, brown them for about 3 minutes on each side. Add half the wine and simmer for about 2 minutes. Transfer the chops to an ovenproof dish and place in the oven to keep warm.

2 Dice the bacon. Peel the onion and slice into thin rings. Peel and finely chop the garlic. Halve and pit the olives. Skin and deseed fresh tomatoes (page 41, Step 3) or drain canned ones, and chop coarsely. Wash, dry, and finely chop the parsley.

3 Heat the remaining oil in the pan, add the bacon, onion, and garlic, and sauté for a few minutes over medium heat. Add the olives, tomatoes, and bay leaf to the pan, and season with salt and pepper. Cover, and cook for about 10 minutes. Remove the bay leaf. Add the rest of the white wine and continue to cook, uncovered, until the sauce begins to thicken.

4 Transfer the chops, and any juices, from the oven to the pan containing the sauce. Sprinkle the chopped parsley over the meat, cover the pan, and cook over very low heat for about 15 minutes.

5 Meanwhile, hard-boil the egg, peel, and chop it. Arrange the pork chops on a dish. Add the chopped egg to the sauce and pour the sauce over the meat. Serve hot.

Fegato alla veneziana

Simple • Veneto   **Calf's Liver with Onions**   *Serves 4*

14 oz. onions
1 small bunch flat-leafed parsley
(about 1 oz.)
4 fresh sage leaves
1 lb. 2 oz. calf s liver
all-purpose flour for coating
4 tbsp. butter
4 tbsp. olive oil
1 cup meat broth
salt
freshly ground white pepper

Preparation time: 30 minutes

380 cal. per serving

1 Peel the onions and cut them into thin rings. Wash the parsley and sage leaves and shake them dry. Finely chop the parsley. Carefully remove membrane and any connective tissues from the calf's liver; rinse and pat dry. With a sharp knife, cut into thin strips and coat the strips with all-purpose flour.

2 In a skillet, heat half the butter and half the olive oil. Briefly sauté the sage in the fat, then remove and set aside. Add the onion rings and sauté over low heat for about 15 minutes, stirring frequently, until soft and transparent. Moisten from time to time with a little of the broth. Turn them out onto a plate and keep warm.

3 Heat the rest of the butter and oil in the pan and brown the liver on both sides. Add the remaining meat broth and simmer gently for 2 to 4 minutes until

all the liquid has evaporated. Return the onions to the pan and season with salt and pepper.

4 Serve hot, garnished with the parsley and reserved sage leaves and accompanied, if you like, by polenta (recipe, page 71).

Wine: Choose a young, dry red wine, such as a Tuscan Merlot.

Variation:
Fegato al vino bianco
(Calf's Liver in White Wine)
Heat 4 tbsp. butter in a skillet and brown 1¼ lb. sliced calf's liver for 1 to 2 minutes. Mix 1 cup dry white wine with 1 tbsp. all-purpose flour in a bowl, pour onto the liver and braise for 2 to 4 minutes. Season with salt and pepper.

Saltimbocca alla romana

Quick and easy • Rome   **Scallops of Veal with Ham and Sage**   *Serves 4*

8 thin veal scallops
(about 1¼ lb.)
⅓ cup butter
8 fresh sage leaves
8 slices prosciutto
salt
freshly ground white pepper
4 tbsp. Marsala or white wine
Preparation time: 20 minutes
380 cal. per serving

1 Preheat the oven to 275 degrees. Beat the scallops flat and set aside. Heat the butter in a large skillet until it becomes frothy. Add the sage leaves and toss in the butter for about 1 minute. Remove and keep warm in the oven.

2 Add the prosciutto to the pan, and sauté for about 2 minutes. Remove, and keep warm with the sage.

3 Add the scallops to the same pan, and fry them in the butter for 2 minutes on each side. Season with a little salt and pepper. Transfer them to a warmed serving dish; top each one with a slice of prosciutto and a sage leaf. Cover and keep warm in the oven.

4 Add the wine and 1 tbsp. water to the pan juices. Bring to the boil, stirring well, and pour over the Saltimbocca. Serve immediately, accompanied by crusty white bread and salad in season.

Wine: Choose a fresh, light white wine from Lazio – such as Frascati, or Est! Est!! Est!!! – or a light red, such as Rosso di Montalcino from Tuscany.

Note: *Saltimbocca* literally means "jump in the mouth".

Sage

The distinctive, slightly bitter taste of sage adds a spicy note to many Italian recipes, from soups and pastas to meat dishes and stews. It goes particularly well with veal (*below*) and liver, as in Fegato alla veneziana (page 95).

The flavor and the sharp scent are held in a volatile oil contained in the silvery-green, oval leaves of the sage plant, *Salvia officinalis*, which is only fully released through cooking. Both fresh and dried sage, which crumbles easily, are strongly flavored and should be used sparingly.

Fresh sage can be picked most of the year, but it is at its best – especially for drying – in late spring and early summer, just before the purple or white flowers appear.

The name Salvia comes from the Latin *salvus*, meaning "healthy," and the plant has long been credited with medicinal properties. In the first century AD, the ancient Greek physician and pharmacologist Dioscorides, whose work remained influential in Europe until the end of the 15th century, recommended sage as a styptic and as a treatment for fever and kidney stones. Such were its reputed powers that a superstitious belief suggested that sage could provide immortality.

Coniglio fritto

Fried Rabbit in Batter

Not difficult • Tuscany

Serves 6

1 egg
6 tbsp. all-purpose flour
½ cup milk
salt
1 tender young rabbit (about
3 lb. 5 oz.) cut into 12 pieces
freshly ground black pepper
vegetable oil for frying
2 lemons

Preparation time: 50 minutes
(plus 1 hour standing time)

450 cal. per serving

1 Beat the egg in a bowl and stir in 5 tbsp. of the all-purpose flour. Gradually stir in the milk to make a creamy, medium-thick batter. Season with a little salt. Leave to stand for about 1 hour.

2 Rinse the rabbit pieces under running water, removing splinters of bone, and pat dry with kitchen paper. Season with salt and pepper. Sprinkle the pieces with the remaining all-purpose flour and dip each one in the batter.

3 In a heavy pan, heat enough oil to cover the base by about ¼ inch. Add the rabbit pieces a few at a time and fry them for 5 to 10 minutes over high heat, turning occasionally, until lightly browned all over. Reduce the heat to medium, and continue to cook for about 20 to 30 minutes, turning frequently, until the meat is tender.

4 Wash the lemons in hot water, rub dry and cut into wedges. Thoroughly drain the cooked rabbit pieces on kitchen paper. Arrange them on a warmed dish and garnish with the lemon wedges. Serve hot.

Agnello in umido

Braised Lamb with Green Peas

Fairly easy • Abruzzi

Serves 4

4 garlic cloves
2 ¼ lb. boned leg of lamb
in one piece
1 sprig rosemary
salt
freshly ground black pepper
2 oz. smoked bacon
6 tbsp. olive oil
½ cup dry white wine
1 ¾ cups ripe tomatoes, or canned
tomatoes
1 small bunch flat-leafed parsley
(about 1 oz.)
1 tsp. fresh thyme, or ½ tsp
dried thyme
2 ¼ lb. freshly shelled, or
frozen, peas
Preparation time: 2 hours
950 cal. per serving

1 Peel the garlic and cut into slivers. Briefly rinse the lamb under running water and pat dry. With the point of a knife, cut small slits at regular intervals in the meat and insert garlic slivers and rosemary leaves. Season with salt and pepper.

2 Dice the bacon. Heat the oil in a heavy pan. Add the bacon and lamb and brown for about 15 minutes. Add the wine and continue to cook, uncovered, until the wine evaporates.

3 Skin and deseed fresh tomatoes (page 41, Step 3), or drain canned tomatoes and reserve the juice. Chop the tomatoes. Wash, dry, and finely chop the parsley. Add the tomatoes and parsley to the lamb. Season with salt and the thyme. Tightly cover the pan and braise for about 30 to 40 minutes over low heat, until tender. Add a little water or reserved tomato juice if the meat becomes too dry.

4 Remove the meat and keep warm. If using fresh peas, add them to the pan juices and simmer over low heat for about 15 minutes. Defrosted frozen peas need only about 5 minutes.

5 Cut the lamb into pieces and arrange on a warmed dish. Pour over the pan juices and peas, and serve hot.

Wine: A dry Sardinian red wine, such as an Oliena Cannonau or a Monica, goes well with lamb.

Note: Lamb chops can be substituted, but may need less time to cook.

Lepre in umido

Braised Hare

More complex • Tuscany *Serves 4*

2 ¼ *lb. saddle of hare*
cut into 8 pieces
1 tbsp. wine vinegar
1 large onion
2 carrots
2 garlic cloves
2 sticks celery
2 slices rindless bacon
1 ½ cups fresh mixed mushrooms,
(including porcini, if available)
salt
3 tbsp. olive oil
2 sprigs rosemary
4 tbsp. butter
1 cup dry red wine
2 cups sieved tomatoes
2 bay leaves
freshly ground black pepper

Preparation time: 2 hours

640 cal. per serving

1 Put the hare in a bowl and pour on just enough cold water, mixed with the vinegar, to cover. Marinate for about 30 minutes.

2 Meanwhile, peel the onion and cut into thin rings. Peel and finely chop the carrots and garlic. Trim, string, and finely chop the celery. Cut the bacon into ¼ inch strips. Trim and briefly wash the mushrooms and chop coarsely.

3 Remove the hare from the water, rinse briefly, pat dry, then rub the portions with salt. Heat the oil in a large, heavy pan. Put in the hare and sauté for about 15 minutes until well browned all over. Add the bacon and onion and sauté briefly, then add the carrots, garlic, celery, and rosemary. Cook for 5 minutes. Meanwhile, melt

the butter in a skillet and cook the mushrooms for about 5 minutes.

4 Add half the red wine to the hare and cook, uncovered, over medium heat until it evaporates, turning the meat several times. Add the mushrooms and, little by little, the sieved tomatoes and remaining wine. Then add the bay leaves and season with salt and pepper. Cover, and braise over very low heat for about 1 hour, until the meat is tender.

5 Remove the hare and rosemary sprigs from the pan. Arrange the meat on a warmed serving dish, topped with the sauce. Serve immediately.

Note: Presoaked dried mushrooms can be substituted for the fresh ones.

Rosemary

Rosemary is a favorite herb in Italian cooking. Used fresh or dried, it goes well with meat – particularly lamb and veal – poultry, game, strongly flavored fish, and beans, and it is also used to flavor vinegar and olive oil.

The bushy, evergreen shrub grows wild on the rocky hillsides of the Mediterranean regions, where it can reach a height of up to seven feet. The flowers are lavender-blue or sometimes white and bloom in early spring (above, right). The plant's leathery, needle-like leaves have an

intense aroma, mildly reminiscent of camphor and, when the wind is in the right direction, the fragrance wafts up to 18 miles out to sea.

Rosemary – the plant's Latin name *Rosamarinus* means "sea dew" – is

traditionally known as the herb of remembrance. The ancient Romans dedicated it to Venus, goddess of love, and valued it both as a culinary and medicinal plant, a natural remedy for a variety of ailments.

Tacchino al latte

Fairly easy • Tuscany **Turkey Braised in Milk**   **Serves 4**

*2 ½ lb. boneless turkey meat
(breast or leg)
1 onion • 2 carrots
1 stick celery
4 garlic cloves
4 to 6 fresh sage leaves
4 tbsp. olive oil
6 tbsp. butter • salt
freshly ground white pepper
3 tbsp. brandy
2 cups porcini or portobello
mushrooms
1 cup milk*

Preparation time: 1 ½ hours

500 cal. per serving

1 Rinse the turkey and pat dry with kitchen paper. Cut the meat into bite-sized pieces. Peel and finely chop the onion and carrots. Wash, string, and finely chop the celery. Peel the garlic cloves. Wash and dry the sage leaves.

2 In a heavy pan, heat the oil with the whole garlic cloves. Add half the butter and briefly fry the sage leaves. Remove the garlic. Add the turkey and lightly brown it all over. Add the vegetables and season with salt and pepper, and continue to cook, stirring constantly.

3 Dilute the brandy with ½ cup water and pour some over the meat. Cover

the pan and braise the turkey over low heat for 45 to 55 minutes, adding more of the liquid as necessary, until the meat is tender. Meanwhile, trim, rinse, and slice the mushrooms, and cook them in the remaining butter in another pan. Preheat the oven to 275 degrees.

4 Pour the milk over the turkey and stir until the sauce begins to thicken. Transfer the pieces of turkey to an ovenproof dish and keep warm in the oven. Add the vegetable sauce to the mushrooms and simmer for about 10 minutes. Pour the mushroom sauce over the turkey pieces.

Faraona con patate

Fairly easy • Emilia-Romagna **Guinea Fowl with Potatoes and Shallots**   **Serves 4**

*8 tbsp. olive oil
3 fresh sage leaves
1 small oven-ready guinea fowl
(chicken is a handy substitute)
(about 2 ¼ lb.) with liver
all-purpose flour for coating
salt
3 slices smoked bacon
2 garlic cloves
1 small orange or mandarin
freshly ground black pepper
10 ½ oz. small new potatoes
10 ½ oz. shallots
1 sprig rosemary*

Preparation time: 1 ½ hours

620 cal. per serving

1 Heat 1 tbsp. of the oil in a small skillet and briefly fry 1 sage leaf to flavor the oil. Lightly flour the liver and brown briefly on each side. Season with a little salt and leave to cool.

2 Dice 1 slice bacon. Peel and mince the garlic. Finely chop the remaining sage. Peel the orange or mandarin and chop the flesh into small pieces. Finely chop the cooled liver. Mix everything together in a bowl.

3 Rinse and dry the guinea fowl. Rub inside and out with salt and pepper. Fill with the stuffing and sew up the opening. Cover the breast with the remaining bacon (secure with toothpicks, if necessary).

4 Preheat the oven to 425 degrees. Scrape, wash, and slice the potatoes. Peel and halve the shallots. Pour 3 tbsp. of the oil into a roasting pan and arrange the sliced potatoes in the bottom. Sprinkle with 3 tbsp. of the oil and season with salt and pepper. Sprinkle rosemary leaves over the potatoes. Arrange the shallots round the edge. Brush the bird with the remaining oil and place in the center of the pan, breast upward. Roast in the center of the oven for 50 minutes to 1 hour, until the skin is crisp and the wings pull away easily.

Wine: Serve with a light white wine, such as a Galestro from Tuscany, or a light-bodied red wine.

Pollo con le olive

Not difficult · Siena

Braised Chicken with Olives

Serves 4

1 oven-ready chicken
(about 3 lb. 5 oz.)
salt
freshly ground black pepper
10 fresh sage leaves
3 garlic cloves
4 tbsp. olive oil
½ cup dry white wine
1 lb. 5 oz. ripe plum tomatoes, or
canned tomatoes
⅔ cup plump black olives

Preparation time: 1 hour

500 cal. per serving

1 Divide the chicken into 4 pieces. Wash and dry, removing any splinters of bone. Season with salt and pepper. Wash and dry the sage and finely chop 6 of the leaves. Peel the garlic and cut into slivers.

2 Heat the olive oil in a heavy pan. Toss the garlic and chopped sage in the oil, then add the chicken quarters and lightly brown them on all sides. Moisten with a little of the wine.

3 Skin and deseed fresh tomatoes (page 41, Step 3), or drain canned ones. Finely chop the tomatoes and add them to the chicken. Sauté for a few minutes, then add the rest of the wine. Cover the pan and cook over low heat for about 15 minutes. Halve and pit the olives and add them to the pan. Cover, and cook for a further 15 minutes, until the chicken is tender.

4 Arrange the chicken quarters on a warmed serving dish, pour the sauce over them, and garnish with the remaining sage leaves. Serve with crusty bread.

Wine: A light red wine from Piedmont, such as a Dolcetto d'Alba, is an excellent accompaniment to this dish.

Chicken Fricassee

Fairly easy · Lazio

Fricassea di pollo

Serves 4

1 corn-fed chicken (about 2 ¼ lb.)
salt
freshly ground white pepper
all-purpose flour for coating
1 large white onion
3 tbsp. butter
4 tbsp. olive oil
½ cup dry white wine
1 bay leaf
1 cup chicken broth
2 egg yolks
juice of 1 lemon
parsley (optional)

Preparation time: 1 ½ hours

550 cal. per serving

1 Wash the chicken inside and out, and dry with kitchen paper. Using poultry shears or a sharp kitchen knife, cut it into 10 to 12 pieces. Remove any bone splinters, season with salt and pepper, and coat with all-purpose flour.

2 Peel the onion and cut into thin rings. Heat the butter and olive oil in a heavy pan. Add the chicken and sauté until lightly browned on all sides. Transfer from the pan to a plate. Preheat the oven to 275 degrees.

3 Add the onion rings to the pan and sauté until transparent, then stir in the wine. Add the bay leaf and continue to cook until the sauce thickens. Pour in half the broth, return to the boil, and cook for 2 minutes.

4 Return the chicken to the pan, cover, and cook over low heat for 20 to 30 minutes, occasionally adding a little of the broth and returning to the boil each time. Remove from the heat, transfer the chicken to an ovenproof dish, and keep warm in the oven.

5 Whisk the egg yolks with the lemon juice and add them to the pan juices, stirring vigorously. Season with salt and pepper. Warm through over low heat, but do not allow to boil. Serve the chicken on warmed plates, covered with the sauce and, if you like, garnished with a few parsley leaves.

Piccioni ripieni al forno

Roast Stuffed Squab

Not difficult • Umbria   *Serves 4*

**4 small, oven-ready squab,
with livers and hearts
(or chicken livers, if unavailable)
salt
freshly ground black pepper
4 slices pancetta or bacon
6 tbsp. olive oil**

**For the stuffing:
1 ½ tbsp. butter
½ cup dry white wine
2 large bread rolls, crusts removed
½ cup milk
1 small bunch parsley (about 1 oz.)
4 garlic cloves
1 thick slice ham (about 1 ½ oz.)
1 egg
freshly grated nutmeg**

Preparation time: 1 ½ hours

790 cal. per serving

1 Wash the squab under running water, then dry. Pull out any feather ends remaining in the skin. Season inside and out with salt and pepper. Trim the livers and hearts, removing connective tissue, wash and pat dry.

2 For the stuffing, melt the butter in a skillet and briefly sauté the livers and hearts. Pour in half the wine, cover and braise for about 10 minutes. Meanwhile, soak the bread rolls in the milk. Wash, dry, and chop the parsley. Peel and chop the garlic. Dice the ham. Whisk the egg. Preheat the oven to 400 degrees.

3 Chop the livers and hearts and mix together with the parsley, garlic, diced ham, and egg. Season with salt, pepper, and nutmeg. Squeeze the bread dry, chop finely, add to the rest of the ingredients, and knead well together.

4 Stuff the birds with the mixture. Sew up the openings or fasten with toothpicks. Wrap a slice of pancetta around each squab. Pour the oil into a roasting pan and place the squab in the pan. Roast in the center of the oven for about 1 hour, depending on the size of the birds, until golden-brown, basting with the remaining wine from time to time.

5 Remove the threads or toothpicks and, if you like, carefully cut the squab in half with poultry shears. Place them on a warmed serving dish. Serve with roast potatoes.

Wine: An excellent choice would be a dry red wine from Tuscany, such as a Vino Nobile di Montepulciano or a Chianti Classico.

Quaglie al tegame

Fairly easy • Veneto **Braised Quail with Raisins and Spinach** *Serves 4*

8 plump oven-ready quail
salt
freshly ground black pepper
8 fresh sage leaves
8 garlic cloves
8 tbsp. raisins
4 tbsp. olive oil
½ cup dry white wine
4 cups fresh spinach

Preparation time: 50 minutes

600 cal. per serving

1 Rinse the quail, dry with kitchen paper, and remove any remaining feather ends. Lightly season inside and out with salt and pepper.

2 Wash and dry the sage leaves. Peel the garlic cloves. Stuff each quail with 1 sage leaf, 1 garlic clove, and 1 tbsp. raisins. Close the abdominal cavities and secure with toothpicks.

3 Heat the olive oil in a large, heavy pan, add the quail, and cook for about 5 minutes until lightly brown all over.

4 Pour on half the wine, cover, and braise the birds over low heat for 20 to 30 minutes, basting with the remaining wine from time to time. Then remove the lid, and continue to cook for about 5 minutes, or until the sauce begins to thicken.

5 Meanwhile, remove the stems from the spinach and wash thoroughly. Place the wet spinach in a saucepan, cover, and steam over low heat for about 1 minute, or until the leaves wilt. Drain, squeeze well, and chop.

6 Remove the quail from the pan, take out the toothpicks, and keep warm. Add the spinach to the pan and toss it briefly in the quail juices. Season with salt and pepper. Serve the quail with the pan juices, accompanied by the spinach.

Wine: This dish goes well with a dry red wine from the Basilicata, such as the excellent Aglianico del Vulture.

CRONACHE ITALIANE

re al grigiore del mercato

nte forti   Il boom de

ine contra crisi   Bici

icam mi colori   E' l'

CONTORNI

Vegetables, salad greens, and fruits are among Italy's greatest culinary treasures and are treated accordingly. Grouped together as contorni, or side dishes, they accompany Italian *secondi piatti*, served on separate plates to keep their flavors intact. But many of these dishes – *Caponata siciliana, Malanzane alla parmigiana*, or *Bagna cauda*, for instance – also take pride of place as appetizers or entrées.

However they are served, the rules are the same. Only the best and freshest vegetables should appear, and they will be at their finest if treated simply. On hot days, *insalata mista*, a colorful mixed salad, is all that is necessary. For cooked dishes, vegetables are best steamed to keep their flavors and vitamins intact.

Italians are especially fond of edible vegetables and herbs grown in the wild. These include a range of wild mushrooms; delicate wild asparagus and fennel; rosemary and oregano; and many different leaves and flowers for mixing in salads.

First among the cultivated vegetables are eggplant, closely followed by bell peppers, spinach, broccoli, zucchini, peas, celery, and carrots. Tomatoes – really a fruit – and artichokes are grown on a large scale. Many regions have their own characteristic vegetables; white beans, for instance, appear on nearly every Tuscan menu.

Pomodori ripieni in insalata

Not difficult • Calabria **Stuffed tomatoes** *Serves 8*

8 large, ripe, firm beefsteak
tomatoes
salt
4 eggs
²⁄₃ cup tuna canned in oil
1 ½ cups mozzarella cheese
1 small bunch basil (about 1 oz.)
8 green olives
3 anchovy fillets canned in oil
freshly ground black pepper
4 tbsp. virgin olive oil
4 large black olives

Preparation time: 40 minutes

260 cal. per serving

1 Wash the tomatoes and slice off the tops. With a teaspoon, carefully remove the seeds and discard. Scoop out the flesh, chop finely, and set aside. Sprinkle the insides of the tomatoes with a little salt, and stand them upside down to drain off any surplus liquid. Hard-boil the eggs.

2 Thoroughly drain the tuna and flake it into small pieces. Dice the mozzarella. Remove the stems and wash the basil leaves, pat dry, and finely chop half of them. Pit the green olives and cut into rings. Drain the anchovies and chop them into small pieces. Shell and dice the eggs. Place all these ingredients in a large bowl, add the reserved tomato flesh, and mix lightly. Season with salt and pepper.

3 Sprinkle the insides of the tomato shells with 3 tbsp. of the olive oil. Fill them with the tuna mixture and arrange on individual plates. Halve the black olives and pit them. Garnish the tomatoes with the olive halves and remaining basil, and sprinkle with the remaining olive oil. Serve as a side dish or starter.

Variation:
Rice can be used instead of tuna for the filling. Mix 8 to 10 tbsp. cold, boiled rice with 1 tsp. dried oregano and some chopped parsley. Omitting the tuna and basil, add the other ingredients as above.

Tomatoes

Originally a wild Andean plant, the tomato was first cultivated by the ancient Aztec empires of Peru, whence it was introduced to southern Italy in the 16th century. Over the centuries, tomatoes became a vital ingredient in a range of Italian dishes.

It was the Italians, in fact, who developed tomatoes as we know them. The original tomato was yellow – hence its Italian name, pomodori or "golden apples" – unlike the bright red fruits of today. Nowadays, Italian cookery uses a variety of tomatoes, including the large beefsteak tomato, the round cherry or salad tomato, and the elongated plum tomato, most frequently used for sauces and canning.

Plum tomatoes are grown primarily in the south of the country and dominate its cookery. The high-summer start of the tomato harvest in Sicily, for example, is the occasion for a get-together, when local women join forces to preserve the gathered fruit, which is peeled and bottled whole or puréed. The thick-skinned *pomodori a grapolo* are threaded and hung by their stems to dry well into the winter. Tomatoes are also preserved by being dried in the sun (*above*). Dried tomatoes, *pomodori secchi*, eaten in olive oil, have an incomparable, spicy flavor.

Peperonata

Peppers with tomatoes and onions   *Serves 4*

1 lb. 2 oz. ripe plum tomatoes
1 lb. 2 oz. red bell peppers
1 lb. 2 oz. yellow bell peppers
2 large white onions
6 tbsp. olive oil
salt
1 small bunch basil (about 1 oz.)

Preparation time: 50 minutes

220 cal. per serving

1 Plunge the tomatoes quickly in boiling water, remove, and skin. Chop them into small pieces.

2 Wash the peppers and cut off the stem ends. Cut each pepper in half and remove the seeds and white ribs. Slice into strips about ¾ inch wide. Peel and finely slice the onions.

3 Heat 5 tbsp. of the olive oil in a heavy saucepan and sauté the onions until transparent.

4 Add the peppers, sauté for about 5 minutes, then add the chopped tomatoes. Season with salt.

5 Stir in about ½ cup water. Cover the pan and simmer gently over low heat for about 35 minutes, stirring occasionally. If the mixture becomes too dry, add more water as required. Meanwhile, stem, wash and dry the basil.

6 Garnish the peperonata with the basil leaves and sprinkle with the remaining olive oil. Serve hot.

Note: For more flavor, add 1 to 2 tbsp. capers and/or black olives. Peperonata is also good served cold, dressed with a little wine vinegar.

Fagioli all'uccelletto

White Beans with Tomatoes and Sage   *Serves 4 to 6*

1¾ cups dried cannellini, or navy beans (or 2¾ cups fresh white beans in their shells)
salt
1¾ cups tomatoes, fresh or canned
10 fresh sage leaves
4 garlic cloves
6 tbsp. virgin olive oil
freshly ground black pepper

Preparation time: 2 hours (plus bean-soaking time)

480 cal. per serving (if serving 6)

1 If using dried beans, soak in 1 quart water for 8 hours or overnight. Then drain, place in a pan with 1 quart fresh water, add salt, and bring to the boil without covering the pan. Boil briskly for a few minutes, then cover, and simmer over low heat for about 1 ½ hours until tender. If using fresh beans, shell and cook immediately for about 1 hour.

2 Skin and deseed fresh tomatoes (page 41, Step 3). Drain canned tomatoes. Chop the tomatoes. Wash the sage leaves and pat dry. Peel the garlic and slice very finely.

3 Heat 4 tbsp. of the olive oil in a heavy saucepan, add the garlic and sage leaves, and sauté briefly. Drain the cooked beans and add to the pan. Season with salt and plenty of pepper and simmer for about 5 minutes.

4 Add the tomatoes, cover the pan and simmer over low heat for about 15 minutes. Sprinkle with the rest of the olive oil and serve hot.

Caponata siciliana

Sicilian Vegetables

1 lb. 9 oz. eggplant
salt
2 medium-sized white onions
2 sticks celery
1 lb. 2 oz. fresh or canned
tomatoes
2 tbsp. green olives
4 anchovy fillets canned in oil
10 tbsp. olive oil
freshly ground black pepper
all-purpose flour for coating
3 tbsp. white wine vinegar
3 tsp. sugar
1 tbsp. capers
1 tbsp. pine nuts
basil leaves for garnish (optional)

Preparation time: 1½ hours
(plus cooling time)

240 cal. per serving
(if serving 6)

1 Remove the eggplant stalks. Wash the eggplant and cut lengthwise into slices ½ inch thick (see page 118, Step 1). Sprinkle the slices evenly with salt, place in a large sieve or colander, and leave to stand for 1 hour to draw off the bitter juices. Rinse thoroughly; pat dry with kitchen paper, and dice.

2 While the eggplant is sweating, peel the onions and slice them into thin rings. Trim the celery, wash thoroughly, and string it. Cut into pieces about 1 inch long.

3 Skin and deseed the fresh tomatoes (page 41, Step 3). Drain canned tomatoes. Chop the tomatoes into small pieces. Stone and coarsely chop the olives, and drain the anchovies.

4 Heat 2 tbsp. of the olive oil in a heavy skillet. Sauté the onions until

transparent, then add the celery and sauté for about 5 minutes (*above*). Season with salt and pepper. Transfer to a bowl and set aside.

5 In a heavy skillet, heat 6 tbsp. of the olive oil until very hot. Lightly coat the diced eggplant in all-purpose flour and fry a few at a time for 8 to 10 minutes

until golden brown (*above*). Remove from the pan with a slotted spoon and leave to drain on kitchen paper.

6 Wipe the pan clean and heat the remaining oil. Quickly sauté the anchovy fillets. Add the tomatoes and, after about 7 minutes, the cooked onions, celery, and eggplant. Combine the vinegar and sugar, and pour into the pan. Continue to cook over a low heat for 10 to 15 minutes, stirring frequently. Add the olives, capers, and pine nuts and mix well. Season with salt and pepper.

7 Transfer the *Caponata* to a serving bowl and leave to stand in a cool place. If you like, garnish with basil leaves. Serve as a side dish or starter. Variation: Add 1 tbsp. raisins, soaked in lukewarm water for about 15 minutes and drained, to the *Caponata* with the onions and celery.

Note: *Caponata* makes an excellent accompaniment to *Braciole di maiale alle olive* (recipe, page 94). It also serves as a appetizer when served with toasted white bread, or as an entrée with Parma ham and pecorino cheese.

Carciofi fritti

Fried Artichokes

Fairly easy • Tuscany

Serves 4

2 eggs
5 tbsp. all-purpose flour
salt
4 tbsp. milk
8 young, fleshy artichokes
juice of 1 lemon
½ cup olive oil
freshly ground black pepper
2 lemons for garnish

Preparation time: 30 minutes
(plus up to 1 hour resting time)

240 cal. per serving

1 In a mixing bowl, whisk the eggs with the all-purpose flour and season with salt. Stir vigorously to make a medium-thick batter, adding the milk a little at a time, if required. Let the batter rest for about an hour.

2 Meanwhile, break off the stalks of the young artichokes. Pull off the tough outer leaves and, with a sharp knife, trim the tips of the rest. Cut the artichokes lengthwise into quarters and remove the purple leaves and prickly chokes. Immediately put the prepared artichokes into a bowl of cold water mixed with the lemon juice, until you are ready to cook.

3 Heat the olive oil in a skillet. Drain the quartered artichokes and dip them in the batter one by one. Put them in the skillet a few at a time and fry on all sides until crisp. Lower the heat and continue to cook for a further 5 to 6 minutes.

4 Drain the artichokes thoroughly on kitchen paper. Season with salt and pepper. Cut each lemon into eight wedges. Arrange the artichokes on a serving dish with the lemon wedges and serve hot.

Variation:
The batter can also be used to fry a mixture of 9 oz. sliced zucchini and 9 oz. blanched cauliflower florets.

Note: Only young artichokes are suitable for this dish.

Asparagi al prosciutto

Baked Asparagus Wrapped in Prosciutto

3 lb. 5 oz. green asparagus
salt
5 tbsp. butter
4 slices fontina or Gouda cheese
16 slices prosciutto, or rindless bacon slices
4 tbsp. freshly grated Parmesan cheese
freshly ground white pepper

Preparation time: 1 ½ hours

480 cal. per serving

1 Snap the woody bottoms from the asparagus spears and peel each spear. Wash the asparagus and, using fine kitchen thread, tie them into bundles of several spears each. Bring 3 quarts salted water to the boil in a narrow cooking pot tall enough for the asparagus to stand upright (the tips should not be covered by the water). Add the asparagus bundles, cover the pan, and cook for about 5 to 10 minutes, or until just tender.

2 Meanwhile, preheat the oven to 400 degrees. Grease an ovenproof dish with half the butter. Dice the fontina or Gouda cheese. Remove the asparagus from the water. Rinse them in ice-cold water to stop the cooking, and drain on a clean cloth. Remove the thread.

3 Divide the asparagus into 8 portions, and wrap each serving in 2 slices of prosciutto or bacon, leaving the tips exposed. Arrange the bundles in two layers in the dish, topping each layer with diced cheese. Dot with flakes of the remaining butter.

4 Cover with aluminum foil and bake in the oven for about 8 minutes. Remove the foil, sprinkle with the Parmesan and bake, uncovered, for a further 7 minutes. Season with pepper and serve hot.

Note: Green asparagus must be completely fresh and crisp. When buying asparagus, especially if prepackaged, check spear ends for signs of dryness. If using white asparagus, peel all the skin and cut off the woody ends. Asparagus dries out quickly and should be prepared just before cooking.

Melanzane alla parmigiana

More complex • Parma　　**Eggplant Baked with Cheese**　　*Serves 4 to 6*

2 ¼ *lb. eggplant*
salt
1 lb. 5 oz. fresh or canned
tomatoes
1 carrot
1 stick celery
1 medium-sized onion
2 garlic cloves
1 bunch basil (about 1 oz.)
virgin olive oil
freshly ground black pepper
1 small, fresh chili pepper
2 eggs
all-purpose flour for coating
10 ½ oz. mozzarella cheese
1 ½ cups freshly grated Parmesan
cheese

Preparation time: about 2 hours
(plus cooling time)

400 cal. per serving
(if serving 6)

1 Remove the eggplant stems and cut the eggplant lengthwise into slices about ½ inch thick (*above*). Sprinkle with salt, place in a sieve or colander, and leave to stand for about 1 hour to draw off any bitter juices. Rinse under running water and pat dry.

2 Meanwhile, make the sauce. If using fresh tomatoes, skin and deseed them (page 41, Step 3); or drain the canned tomatoes. Chop the tomatoes. Peel and dice the carrot. Wash and string the celery, and cut it into ¼ inch slices. Peel the onion and garlic cloves and chop them finely. Wash and dry the basil and remove the leaves from the stems.

3 Heat 2 tbsp. olive oil in a heavy saucepan, add the onion, and sauté until transparent. Add the garlic and cook for a few minutes longer, then add the carrot and celery and cook for a few more minutes. Add the chopped tomatoes. Cut half the basil leaves into strips and add to the pan. Season with salt and pepper and add the whole chili pepper. Cover, and simmer over low heat for about 20 minutes. At the end of the cooking time, remove the chili pepper. While the sauce is cooking, hard-boil the eggs.

4 Heat a generous amount of olive oil in two skillets. Coat the eggplant slices in all-purpose flour and fry for 5 to 10 minutes on each side, until golden. Drain the slices on kitchen paper.

5 Preheat the oven to 375 degrees. Drain and dice the mozzarella. Shell and slice the eggs. Brush the inside of an ovenproof dish with 1 tbsp. olive oil.

6 Line the bottom of the dish with a layer of eggplant. Sprinkle with freshly grated Parmesan. Follow with a layer of diced mozzarella and slices of egg and top with tomato sauce (*above*). Continue to layer until all the ingredients are used up, reserving 2 tbsp. of the Parmesan.

7 Bake in the center of the oven for about 35 minutes. Remove from the oven, sprinkle with the reserved Parmesan, and bake for a further 5 to 10 minutes. Leave to cool. Garnish with the remaining basil leaves. Sprinkle with a little olive oil and serve cold.

Wine: This dish goes well with a red wine from Emilia-Romagna, such as the sparkling Lambrusco di Sorbara.

Frittata di patate e zucchini

Simple • Friuli

Potato and Zucchini Omelet

Serves 4

3 medium-sized potatoes
2 zucchini (about 7 oz.)
1 medium-sized onion
6 tbsp. olive oil
salt
½ tsp. fresh rosemary, or ¼ tsp dried rosemary
6 eggs
freshly ground black pepper
1 small bunch parsley (about 1 oz.)

Preparation time: 45 minutes

480 cal. per serving

1 Peel and wash the potatoes, and cut into paper-thin slices. Wash the zucchini, top, and tail them, then cut into slices about ¼ inch thick. Peel and finely chop the onion.

2 Heat 4 tbsp. of the olive oil in a shallow pan. Add first the onion and then the potatoes, and brown them on both sides. Season with salt and rosemary, cover, and cook over low heat for 15 to 20 minutes. Add the zucchini and cook for a further 5 minutes, stirring gently.

3 In a large bowl, whisk the eggs and season with salt and pepper. Transfer the vegetables from the pan to the bowl and mix thoroughly. Heat the remaining olive oil in the same pan. Return the mixture to the pan and cook over low heat for about 5 minutes, or until the omelet sets. Turn it over and cook on the other side, until golden brown.

4 Wash, dry, and mince the parsley. Place the omelet on a serving dish and sprinkle with parsley. Serve hot or cold, with crusty bread.

Crespelle magre di spinaci

Needs care • Emilia-Romagna

Spinach-stuffed Pancakes

Serves 4

For the batter:
1 cup whole-wheat flour
3 eggs
1 cup milk ¥ salt
2 tbsp. butter
freshly ground black pepper

For the filling:
4 cups fresh spinach
salt
4 tbsp. raisins
3 tbsp. virgin olive oil ¥ 2 tbsp. butter
4 slices prosciutto (or ham, if not available)
2 tbsp. pine nuts
7 tbsp. grated Parmesan cheese

Preparation time: 1 hour (plus 30 minutes resting and soaking time)

690 cal. per serving

1 In a mixing bowl, combine the flour, eggs, milk, and a pinch of salt to make a smooth pancake batter. Melt the butter, allow to cool slightly, then fold into the batter. Season with pepper, and leave to rest for about 30 minutes.

2 Meanwhile, trim and wash the spinach and place in a pan. Steam for 1 minute in the water clinging to the leaves. Season with salt. Squeeze thoroughly, reserving the water, then finely chop. Soak the raisins in the spinach water for about 15 minutes.

3 In a heavy pan, heat 2 tbsp. oil and half the butter. Dice the prosciutto and sauté until brown. Add the spinach, pine nuts, and drained raisins and stir. Simmer for 5 minutes, transfer to a bowl and stir in half the Parmesan.

4 Grease a crêpe pan or skillet with a little of the remaining butter. Pour in an eighth of the batter to make a paper-thin pancake, lightly browned on both sides. Spread it with the filling and roll it up. Make seven more pancakes in the same way. Arrange the pancakes on a warmed serving platter. Sprinkle with the remaining Parmesan, season with pepper, and the remaining oil, and serve hot.

Variation: Crespelle al forno
(Spinach-stuffed Pancakes au Gratin)
Preheat the oven to 325 degrees. Prepare filled pancakes as above. Butter an ovenproof dish. Put in 4 pancakes, cover with 3 ½ oz. sliced mozzarella, lay the others on top, cover with Béchamel sauce (page 57) and bake for 10 minutes, until brown.

Bagna cauda

Not difficult • Piedmont   Hot Garlic and Anchovy Sauce with Crudités   *Serves 4 to 6*

1 small, young cauliflower head
1 cup broccoli florets
salt
2 fennel bulbs
1 head young celery
3 bell peppers
(1 red, 1 green, 1 yellow)
6 to 9 carrots
2 heads chicory
1 bunch green onions (scallions)

For the dip:
½ cup anchovies canned in oil
4 to 6 garlic cloves
4 tbsp. butter
¾ cup virgin olive oil

Preparation time: 1 hour

550 cal. per serving
(if serving 6)

1 Trim the cauliflower. Wash the broccoli and trim the woody ends and tough skin of the stalks (*above*). Bring a pan of salted water to the boil and simmer the cauliflower and broccoli for about 5 minutes. Drain thoroughly and divide into florets.

2 Trim the fennel bulbs, removing stalks, any brown patches, and the hard ribs of the outer leaves. Wash thoroughly and cut into quarters. Separate the celery into sticks, string, and wash thoroughly. Cut the sticks into pieces about ¼ inch long.

3 Wash the peppers, halve them, and remove stems, seeds, and ribs. Cut them lengthwise into ½-inch strips. Peel the carrots and cut them into sticks. Trim and wash the chicory and divide it into single leaves. Peel and trim the green onions (scallions) and cut them into short lengths.

4 Drain the anchovies, rinse, and pat dry. Peel and finely chop the garlic. Melt the butter over a low heat in a heavy pan or fondue dish, add the garlic, and sauté briefly. Add the anchovies and mash to a pulp with a fork (*above, right*). Little by little, stir in the olive oil. Heat through for about 5 minutes, stirring frequently, until a creamy

sauce forms. Simmer for a further 5 minutes.

5 Arrange the vegetables on serving dishes. At the table, keep the sauce warm over a heat source such as a plate-warmer or a fondue-burner. The vegetables are eaten with the fingers, with everyone helping themselves and dipping the vegetables in the sauce. Serve with plenty of fresh bread.

Wine: One of Piedmont's foremost red wines, such as a Barolo or Barbera, makes an excellent accompaniment to Bagna cauda.

Variation: Pinzimonio
For a cold, nongarlic alternative, combine ¾ cup olive oil, salt, pepper and, if you like, 2 to 3 tbsp. herb vinegar or lemon juice. Stir thoroughly and serve with the vegetables.

Note: *Bagna cauda* is traditionally served in small stoneware pots. The classic vegetable used is the cardoon (cardi), the blanched stalk of a plant belonging to the thistle family, which is available in the late fall. In spring and early summer, *Bagna cauda* can be served as an appetizer, using any young vegetables in season.

DOLCI

I talians end the meal with cheese and fruit, and – the final touch – a *dolce*, or sweet dessert. Suitable cheeses might include Pecorino, Parmesan, Gorgonzola, or pear-shaped, smoked Scamorza, made from buffalo's milk. Fresh fruit in season is delicious on its own, but it can also be lightly marinated in lemon juice or liqueur, or poached in syrup or wine (*frutta cotta*); and fruit is also an ingredient of many of the wide range of tempting Italian desserts.

Some *dolci*, such as *Cassata alla siciliana*, a rich ricotta and candied fruit cake flavored with chocolate and liqueur, or the classic custard and sponge cake dessert, *Zuppa inglese*, belong to the highlights of Italian culinary art and generally only appear on the table on Sundays, holidays, or large family celebrations – when guests often also bring their own offerings.

For more everyday desserts there are tarts and stewed fruits, creams, and puddings, and a variety of cakes and pastries. And in summer – or indeed, at any time of year – there are ice creams and sorbets in every imaginable delicious flavor.

A glass of Moscato or other sweet wine, such as Marsala or Vin Santo, goes well with many desserts. To end the meal in true Italian style, there is strong, black espresso coffee.

Pesche ripiene

Baked Stuffed Peaches

Fairly easy • Sicily

Serve 4

4 firm, ripe peaches
4 tbsp. almonds
½ cup amaretti (small macaroon cookies) or sponge fingers
powdered (confectioners) sugar
2 slices candied orange
⅓ cup sweet white wine
2 tbsp. butter

Preparation time: 40 minutes

200 cal. per serving

1 Preheat the oven to 350 degrees. Plunge the peaches briefly in boiling water, then remove the skins. Cut the fruit in half, remove the pits, and reserve 3 of them. Spoon a little flesh out of each peach half to make a well for the stuffing. Place the spooned-out flesh in a bowl and mash with a spoon.

2 Crack open the 3 peach pits and remove the kernels. Blanch the almonds in boiling water for about 1 minute, then peel them. Reserve 8 whole almonds for decoration. Crush the rest of the almonds and the peach kernels with a pestle and mortar, or in a food processor.

3 Crumble the amaretti or sponge fingers. Add them and the crushed almonds to the mashed fruit in the bowl. Stir in 1 tsp. powdered (confectioners') sugar. Dice the candied orange slices and add to the mixture. Pour in half the wine and stir the mixture vigorously.

4 Fill the peach halves with the stuffing. Grease an ovenproof dish with the butter. Arrange the peach halves in the dish, decorate each half with a whole almond, and sprinkle with the remaining wine.

5 Bake the peaches in the oven for 15 to 20 minutes. Sprinkle with powdered (confectioners') sugar and serve hot or cold.

Pere ripiene con Gorgonzola

Simple • Lombardy

Pears Stuffed with Gorgonzola

Serves 4

4 large, firm pears
juice of 1 lemon
4 tbsp. mild Gorgonzola cheese
3 tbsp. whipped cream
4 tbsp. ground walnuts

Preparation time: 30 minutes

260 cal. per serving

1 Peel the pears and cut them in half lengthwise, leaving the stem attached to one half of each pear. Remove the cores. With a teaspoon, carefully spoon out a little of the flesh from each half and place in a bowl. Put the pear halves on a dish and sprinkle inside and out with the lemon juice.

2 Stir the Gorgonzola and the whipped cream into the reserved pear flesh and continue to stir until it is creamy.

3 Place 1 tbsp. of the mixture in the hollow of each pear half. Press the pear halves carefully together and

place them on 4 separate plates. Sprinkle with the ground walnuts.

Variation:

Pere cotte (Pears in Syrup)
Peel 2 ¼ lb. firm pears. Put 6 tbsp. water, 4 tbsp. lemon juice, 4 tbsp. sugar, and 1 vanilla pod in a wide, heavy pan. Bring slowly to the boil, stirring until the sugar dissolves. Place all the pears in one layer in the pan. Cover, and simmer for 10 to 20 minutes, turning once, until tender. Remove the vanilla pod and serve cold in the syrup.

Frittelle di riso

Rice Fritters

Serves 4

½ **untreated lemon**
2 **cups milk**
⅓ **cup round-grain rice**
4 **tbsp. unsalted butter**
salt
2 **egg yolks**
2 to 3 **tbsp. all-purpose flour**
2 **tsp. dried yeast**
2 **tbsp. Vin Santo wine, or rum**
finely grated rind of ½ orange
2 **tbsp. sugar**
3 **tbsp. raisins**
1 **egg white**
1 **tbsp. pine nuts**
vegetable oil for frying
powdered (confectioners) sugar

Preparation time 1½ hours

(plus 30 minutes standing time)
380 cal. per serving

1 Wash the lemon in hot water and wipe dry. Using a potato peeler, cut off a few strips of rind.

2 Bring the milk to the boil, add the rice, and cook for about 1 minute, stirring constantly. Add the butter, a pinch of salt, and the lemon rind. Simmer, uncovered, over low heat for 15 to 20 minutes until the rice is soft, stirring occasionally. Remove the pan from the stove and let the rice cool a little. Discard the lemon rind.

3 Stir the egg yolks into the rice. Stir in the all-purpose flour, yeast, and wine or rum. Then stir in the grated orange rind, sugar and raisins. Leave the mixture to rest for about 30 minutes.

4 Beat the egg white until stiff. Add the pine nuts to the rice mixture, then carefully fold in the egg white (*below*).

5 Heat a generous amount of vegetable oil in a skillet. A tablespoon at a time, place the rice mixture in the hot fat

(*above*), and fry until golden-brown on both sides, about 2 minutes. Drain the fritters on kitchen paper and keep warm.

6 Arrange the frittelle on a serving dish and sprinkle with powdered (confectioners') sugar. Serve hot.

Wine: Serve with the rest of the Vin Santo or with a Picolit from Friuli.

Variation:
Dolcini di riso (Little Rice Cakes) Preheat the oven to 350 degrees. Prepare the rice mixture as for the frittelle, but omit the yeast and all-purpose flour, and add 2 tbsp. finely chopped candied peel. Butter 4 or more individual custard cups, sprinkle the insides with bread crumbs, then add the rice mixture. Bake for about 15 minutes and serve warm.

Note: In Italy, frittelle are traditionally eaten on Father's Day.

Latteruolo

Vanilla-flavored Milk Molds

Needs care • Emilia-Romagna   *Serves 4*

1 vanilla pod
1 quart milk
⅔ cup sugar
8 egg yolks
2 egg whites
salt
4 tbsp. butter
juice of ½ lemon
3 tbsp. Marsala

Preparation time: 2 hours

559 cal. per serving

1 Slit the vanilla pod open lengthwise and scrape out the seeds. Put the milk, two-thirds of the sugar, and the vanilla pod in a heavy pan. Bring to the boil and simmer over a low heat for about an hour, stirring occasionally, or until the liquid is reduced by half. Strain through a fine sieve or cheesecloth into a bowl, and leave to cool.

2 Preheat the oven to 350 degrees. Beat the egg yolks until frothy, then stir them carefully into the cooled milk. Whisk the egg whites with a pinch of salt until stiff and fold them carefully into the milk mixture.

3 Use the butter to grease 4 individual nonstick molds or custard cups. Pour in the mixture, cover with aluminum foil and stand them in a bain-marie or ovenproof casserole filled with warm water half way up the sides of the molds. Bake for about 40 minutes. Test with a toothpick. It should come out clean if the mixture has set.

4 Remove the foil from the molds and leave to cool, then unmold them. Dissolve the remaining sugar in a pan with ½ tbsp. water over low heat and stir continuously until it browns. Away from the heat, quickly stir in the lemon juice and Marsala. Pour over the molds.

Bignè di albicocche

Apricot Fritters

More complex • Liguria   *Serves 4*

8 large, firm apricots
3 tbsp. Marsala
1 ½ tbsp. sugar
3 sponge fingers
1 slice candied orange

Batter:
4 tbsp. plain all-purpose flour • salt
1 tsp. sugar
2 egg yolks
2 to 3 tbsp. milk
1 egg white
clarified butter or vegetable oil
1 tbsp. powdered
(confectioners) sugar

**Preparation time: 45 minutes
(plus 1 hour marinating and
standing time)**

240 cal. per serving

1 Plunge the apricots into boiling water, rinse with cold water and skin. With a sharp knife, make an incision along the groove in each fruit and, being careful not to break them in half, remove the stones and reserve.

2 Mix the Marsala with 1½ tbsp. sugar in a deep bowl. Marinate the apricots in the Marsala for about an hour, turning frequently.

3 Meanwhile, make the batter. Sieve the all-purpose flour into a mixing bowl. Add a pinch of salt and the sugar. Stir in the egg yolks and add enough milk to make a thick, smooth batter. Leave the batter to stand for 1 hour.

4 Break open the apricot stones and remove the kernels. Blanch the kernels

briefly in boiling water, peel and chop into small pieces. Crumble the sponge fingers into a shallow bowl or soup plate. Dice the candied orange and stir into the biscuit crumbs together with the apricot kernels. Drain the Marsala marinade from the apricots and stir it into the mixture. Spoon the filling into the apricots and press the openings firmly together to enclose the filling.

5 Whisk the egg white until stiff, then fold it into the batter. Heat a generous amount of butter or vegetable oil in a skillet. Dip the fruit in the batter then fry on all sides until golden-brown. Drain on kitchen paper.

6 Arrange the apricots on a serving dish. Just before serving, sprinkle lightly with the powdered (confectioners') sugar.

Zuppa inglese della mamma

More complex • Tuscany

Chocolate and Egg Custard Charlotte

Serves 6 to 8

4 egg yolks
⅓ cup sugar
2 heaping tbsp. all-purpose flour
6 cups milk
finely grated rind of 1 lemon
⅔ cup cocoa powder
5 tbsp. Alkermes (herb liqueur from Florence)
7 oz. sponge finger cookies

Preparation time: 1 hour (plus 2 hours chilling time)

360 cal. per serving (if serving 8)

1 In a mixing bowl, beat the egg yolks with 2 ½ tbsp. of the sugar until creamy. Add the flour and gradually stir in 1 quart of the milk. Stir in the grated lemon rind, then pour into a heavy saucepan and cook over low heat for 5 to 6 minutes, stirring constantly, until it forms a creamy custard. Remove from the heat and set aside.

2 In another saucepan, mix the cocoa powder with the remaining sugar and milk. Bring to the boil over low heat, stirring constantly. Simmer for another 5 minutes, until the sauce thickens. Remove from the heat and set aside.

3 Pour the liqueur into a shallow bowl. One by one, dip a third of the sponge fingers briefly in the liqueur, and arrange them in the bottom of a glass serving bowl. Cover with a third of the custard, then a third of the chocolate sauce. Repeat these three layers twice more, ending with the chocolate as a decoration (see below).

4 Leave to chill in the refrigerator for at least 2 hours. The dessert tastes even better if left overnight, allowing all the flavors to mingle.

Note: This simple version of *Zuppa inglese*, a recipe from the author's family, makes an ideal party dessert.

Tiramisù

Fairly easy • Turin **Mascarpone Cream**

3 eggs
4 tbsp. sugar
1 cup mascarpone
1 cup cold, strong black coffee
5 tbsp. white vermouth or Marsala
7 oz. sponge finger cookies
unsweetened cocoa powder, or
grated chocolate for dusting

Preparation time: 30 minutes
(plus 2 hours for chilling)

260 cal. per serving
(if serving 6)

1 Separate the eggs. In a bowl, beat the egg yolks and the sugar until the mixture becomes thick and creamy. Beat the whites separately, until stiff.

2 Add the mascarpone to the egg yolk mixture, a spoonful at a time, and stir into a smooth cream. Finally, fold in the beaten egg whites.

3 Mix the coffee with the vermouth, or Marsala, in a shallow bowl. Briefly dip half the sponge fingers in the liquid, soaking both sides, and arrange in a layer on the bottom of a shallow serving dish. Pour half the mascarpone mixture over the sponge fingers.

4 Dip the remaining sponge fingers in the liquid and arrange on top of the mascarpone cream. Finally, pour over the rest of the mascarpone cream, and smooth the surface.

5 Cover, and chill in the refrigerator for about 2 hours. Before serving, sprinkle generously with cocoa powder (using a small sieve makes this easier), or grated chocolate.

133

Cassata alla siciliana

Complex • Sicily Ricotta Cream Cake

Serves 8 to 10

For the sponge:
6 eggs
1 ½ cups powdered (confectioners) sugar
1 tbsp. vanilla sugar (see note, page 136)
8 tbsp. all-purpose flour
6 tbsp. cornstarch

For the filling:
1 ⅓ cups mixed candied fruits
3 ½ oz. semi-sweet chocolate
2 ¾ cups ricotta
1 ⅔ cups powdered (confectioners) sugar
1 tbsp. maraschino liqueur, or Marsala

Preparation time: 2 hours (plus 4 hours chilling time)

600 cal. per serving (if serving 10)

1 Preheat the oven to 350 degrees. To make the sponge, separate the eggs. In a mixing bowl, beat the yolks with the powdered (confectioners') sugar and vanilla sugars until creamy. In another bowl, beat the whites until stiff, then fold into the yolk mixture. Sift the flour and cornstarch over the mixture and fold in gently. Grease the base of an 8-inch springform pan and line with nonstick baking paper. Pour in the sponge mixture and smooth the surface. Bake for 20 to 25 minutes. Leave to cool for about 1 hour.

2 Meanwhile, make the filling. Chop half the candied fruits. Dice the chocolate. Rub the ricotta through a sieve into a bowl. Dissolve the powdered (confectioners') sugar in 5 tbsp. water and cook briefly to make a syrup. Fold the hot syrup into the ricotta. Add the vanilla sugar and 6 tbsp. of the liqueur and stir until creamy. Set aside 5 tbsp. of the mixture and fold the chopped candied fruits and chocolate into the remainder.

3 Cut the sponge in half horizontally and sprinkle each half with the remaining liqueur. Use one half to line the base of a round mold. Cover with two thirds of the cream mixture, place the other half on top, pour on the rest of the mixture, and smooth the surface.

4 Leave to chill in the refrigerator for about 4 hours, then unmold onto a serving dish. Cover with the reserved ricotta cream and decorate with the remaining candied fruits.

Variation: Add 6 tbsp. mixed nuts (pistachios, walnuts, and pine nuts) to the cream.

Tronco di bosco

Not difficult • Valle d Aosta Chocolate Log

Serves 8 to 10

1 cup butter
4 tbsp. almonds
5 tbsp. powdered (confectioners) sugar
2 egg yolks
7 tbsp. unsweetened cocoa powder
5 ½ oz. sponge finger cookies
5 tbsp. rum

Preparation time: 30 minutes (plus 4 hours chilling time)

450 cal. per serving (if serving 10)

1 Cut the butter into pieces and leave in a warm bowl to soften. Meanwhile, blanch the almonds briefly in boiling water, peel, and chop very finely.

2 Whisk the butter until creamy, adding the sugar a little at a time. In another bowl, whisk the yolks until frothy, then fold them into the butter.

3 Sprinkle the cocoa powder into the butter mixture and stir in thoroughly. Break the sponge fingers into pieces and fold them into the mixture with a wooden spoon. Stir in the almonds and the rum. Rest for about 10 minutes.

4 Unmold the mixture onto a sheet of aluminum foil. Use a spoon to form it into a log shape, then roll up firmly in the foil.

5 Chill in the refrigerator for at least 4 hours. Remove the foil, place the cake on a chilled platter, and cut into slices ½ inch thick. Serve at once, because the cake melts quickly at room temperature. Serve with espresso coffee.

Torta di zucca gialla

Fairly easy • Basilicata
Pumpkin Pie

Serves 8 to 12

2 ½ lb. pumpkin
2 cups milk
8 tbsp. ground almonds
⅓ cup sugar
3 eggs
salt
1 ½ tsp. vanilla-flavored sugar
(see note, right)
grated rind of 1 lemon
2 tbsp. butter
3 tbsp. bread crumbs
powdered (confectioners) sugar
(optional)

Preparation time: 2 hours

**240 cal. per serving
(if serving 12)**

1 Cut the pumpkin in half and use a spoon to remove the seeds and coarse stringy flesh. Cut the halves into wedges, then remove the flesh from the shell and grate it coarsely. Wrap the grated pumpkin in a cloth and squeeze out as much liquid as possible. You should have at least 1 ¼ cups pumpkin flesh.

2 Place the pumpkin in a saucepan with the milk, bring to the boil, then simmer over low heat for about 60 minutes, until the mixture becomes creamy. Mix the ground almonds with the sugar and stir into the cooked pumpkin. Leave to cool.

3 Preheat the oven to 350 degrees. Break the eggs into a bowl with a pinch of salt and beat until frothy. Add the vanilla sugar and lemon rind. Pour the egg mixture into the pumpkin mixture and stir thoroughly.

4 Grease a 10-inch springform pan with the butter and sprinkle with bread crumbs. Pour in the pumpkin mixture, smooth into a 1-inch layer and bake in the oven for about 40 minutes, or until light golden-brown. Leave it to cool, cut into small pieces and serve. If you like, sprinkle with powdered (confectioners') sugar before serving.

Note: Vanilla sugar is sold in jars or packets in some supermarkets and delicatessens. But, if unavailable, it is very easy to flavor your own sugar at home. Just put a vanilla pod into a full jar of superfine sugar, close the lid tightly, and leave for at least a week – the longer you leave it, the stronger the vanilla flavor will be.

Castagne nello sciroppo

Takes time • South Tyrol

Sweet Chestnuts in Syrup

4 lb. 8 oz. medium-sized chestnuts
1 untreated orange
1 untreated lemon
3 cups sugar
¾ cup colorless liquor such as vodka
¾ cup brandy
3 tsp. vanilla sugar (see note, left)
2 cinnamon sticks
10 cloves

Preparation time: 1 ½ hours (plus 4 hours standing time)

1,200 cal. per jar (if 6 jars)

1 Preheat the oven to 475 degrees. Using a sharp knife, make a small incision lengthwise on the plumper side of each nut. Roast on a cookie sheet on the top shelf of the oven for about 30 minutes.

2 Meanwhile, wash the orange and lemon in hot water and wipe dry. Peel them and finely slice the peel. Mix the sugar with 1 quart water in a heavy saucepan, add the sliced peel, and simmer over low heat for about 20 minutes. Leave the syrup to cool.

3 Stir the spirit or vodka and brandy into the syrup. Stir in the vanilla sugar, cinnamon, and cloves. Cover tightly, and leave to stand for at least 4 hours.

4 Shell the chestnuts, keeping them whole as far as possible, and arrange in layers in screw-top or preserving jars. Shake the jars frequently, to fit in as many chestnuts as possible. Pour in the syrup and peel to fill the jars. Close tightly, and store in a cool place. The chestnuts are at their best after 2 to 3 months. Serve as a dessert or with afternoon coffee.

Note: Two sorts of sweet chestnut grow wild in Italy. A heart-shaped variety comes from the forests of the Apennines, while round ones grow in South Tyrol. Fresh chestnuts are available here in the fall.

Suggested Menus

The richness and endless variety of Italian cuisine offers a vast range of possible menu combinations. Many Italians like to combine courses with similar flavors, such as a seafood *antipasto* or *primo piatto* followed by a fish *secondo piatto*. This selection, put together from recipes featured in the book, contains suggested menus to suit every occasion, from quick and simple everyday meals to more elaborate feasts suitable for festive and celebratory occasions.

Quick menus

Mozzarella and Tomatoes (*Mozzarella e pomodori*)	34
Pasta with Sardines and Fennel (*Pasta con le sarde*)	62
Tuna Steaks in Tomato Sauce (*Tonno fresco in umido*)	87
Green Salad	—
Fresh Fruit	—

Spaghetti with Bacon and Eggs (*Spaghetti alla carbonara*)	66
Scallop of Veal with Ham and Sage (*Saltimbocca alla romana*)	96
Radicchio Salad	—
Strawberries Marinated in Lemon Juice	—

Fried Polenta (*Polenta fritta*)	71
Pan-fried Trout (*Trota in padella*)	85
Steamed Spinach	—
Stewed Plums	—

Spaghetti with Tuna Sauce (*Spaghetti al tonno*)	66
Shrimp with Caper Sauce (*Gamberoni allo spiedo*)	81
Mixed Salad	—
Morello Cherries in Syrup* with Vanilla Ice Cream	—

Menus to prepare in advance

Seafood Salad (*Insalata di frutti di mare*)	36
Four Seasons Pizza (*Pizza "quattro stagioni"*)	41
Mixed Salad	—
Fruit Salad	—

Bresaola (dried salt beef)*, with Olive Oil, Lemon Juice and Black Pepper	—
Fish and Vegetable Flan (*Torta di pesce*)	82
Mixed Salad	—
Pears in Syrup (*Pere cotte*)	127

Olives with Orange Peel (*Olive con buccia d'arancio*)	35
Tortellini with Ham and Cream Sauce (*Tortellini al prosciutto e panna*)	58
Cold Veal with Tuna Sauce (*Vitello tonnato*)	90
Parmesan or Pecorino Cheese* and Pears	—

Seasonal menus

Spring

Farfalle with Gorgonzola Sauce (*Farfalle al Gorgonzola*)	61
Veal Scallop, Coated in bread crumbs and Fried	—
Baked Asparagus Wrapped in Prosciutto (*Asparagi al prosciutto*)	117
Fresh Pecorino Cheese*	—
Little Rice Cakes (*Dolcini di riso*)	129

Summer

Risotto with Squid (*Risotto nero alla fiorentina*)	50
Baked Bream with Potatoes (*Orata al forno con patate*)	84
Green Salad	—
Baked Stuffed Peaches (*Pesche ripiene*)	126

Fall

Mushrooms on Toasted Bread (*Funghi sul crostini*)	30
Braised Hare (*Lepre in umido*)	100
Ribbon Egg Noodles Tossed in the Sauce from the Hare, with freshly grated Parmesan Cheese	—
Steamed Swiss Chard and Spinach	—
Assorted Cheeses*	—

Winter

Hot Chicken Liver Canapés (*Crostini de fegato di pollo*)	32
Cabbage Soup with Bread and Cheese (*Zuppa alla valdostana*)	46
Braised Knuckle of Veal (*Ossobuco alla milanese*)	92
Sweet Chestnuts in Syrup (*Castagne nello sciroppo*)	137

Everyday menus

Penne with Chili Sauce (*Penne all'arrabbiata*)	62
Braised Chicken with Olives (*Pollo con le olive*)	105
Peppers with Tomatoes and Onions (*Peperonata*)	112
Fresh Fruit	—

Minestrone with Peas and Pesto (*Minestrone con piscelli e pesto*)	45
Little Potato Pizzas (*Pizzette di patate*)	38
Green Salad	—
Stewed Fruit	—

Saffron Risotto (*Risotto alla milanese*)	52
Braised Knuckle of Veal (*Ossobuco alla milanese*)	92
Peas	—
Pears Stuffed with Gorgonzola (*Pere ripiene con Gorgonzola*)	127

Minestrone Soup (*Minestrone di verdure*)	44
Calf's Liver in White Wine (*Fegato al vino bianco*)	95
Green Salad	—
Stewed Fruit	—

Dinner party menus

Mushroom Salad (*Insalata di funghi*)	30
Rigatoni with Walnut Sauce (*Rigatoni al sugo di noci*)	61
Chicken Fricassee (*Fricassea di pollo*)	105
Mashed Potatoes	—
Fresh Fruits	
Eggplant Baked with Cheese	
(*Melanzane alla parmigiana*)	118
Pork Chops with Black Olives	
(*Braciole di maiale alle olive*)	94
Baked Stuffed Peaches (*Pesche ripiene*)	126
Potato Gnocchi with Ricotta (*Gnocchi di patate*)	68
Fried Rabbit in Batter (*Coniglio fritto*)	98
Fried Artichokes (*Carciofi fritti*)	116
Cheese and fruit	—
Antipasto (hors-d'oeuvre with ham and salami)*	—
Spinach-stuffed Pancakes au Gratin (*Crespelle al forno*)	121
Turkey Braised in Milk (*Tacchino al latte*)	102
Pecorino cheese*	—
Stuffed Tomatoes	
(*Pomodori ripieni in insalata*)	110
Spinach Gnocchi (*Gnocchi verdi*)	68
Cold Veal with Tuna Sauce (*Vitello tonnato*)	90
Ricotta Cream Cake (*Cassata alla siciliana*)	134

Festive menus

Easter

Marinated Fillet of Raw Beef (*Carpaccio del Cipriani*)	30
Mushrooms on Toasted Bread (*Funghi sul crostini*)	30
Tagliatelle with Meat Sauce (*Tagliatelle al ragù*)	57
Braised Lamb with Green Peas (*Agnello in umido*)	98
Guinea Fowl with Potatoes and Shallots	
(*Faraona con patate*)	102
Assorted cheeses*	—
Vanilla-flavored Milk Moulds (*Latteruolo*)	130
Panettone*, or Colomba pasquale* (see Glossary)	—

Christmas

Antipasto (San Daniele ham, coppa and salami)*	—
Meat Broth with Tortellini (*Minestra in brodo*)	—
Buttered Ravioli Stuffed with Spinach	
(*Ravioli al burro*)	55
Roast Stuffed Pigeons (*Piccioni ripieni al forno*)	106
Mashed potatoes	—
Assorted cheeses*	—
Chocolate and Egg Custard Charlotte (*Zuppa inglese*)	132
Panforte* and Panettone* (see Glossary)	—

Meat-based menus

Polenta with Cheese and Truffles (*Polenta con tartufi*)	70
Braised Quail with Raisins and Spinach	
(*Quaglie al tegame*)	107
Rice Fritters (*Frittelle di riso*)	129
Green Lasagne (*Lasagne verdi al forno*)	57
Turkey Braised in Milk (*Tacchino al latte*)	102
Vanilla-flavored Milk Molds (*Latteruolo*)	130
Polenta with Meat Sauce (*Polenta al piatto con ragù*)	70
Calf's Liver with Onions (*Fegato alla veneziana*)	95
Mashed potatoes	—
Mascarpone Cream (*Tiramisù*)	133

Fish-based menus

Seafood Risotto (*Risotto ai frutti di mare*)	51
Stuffed Squid (*Calamari ripieni*)	76
Pears in Syrup (*Pere cotte*)	127
Mussels au Gratin (*Cozze gratinate alla tarantina*)	78
Mixed Fish Stew (*Cacciucco alla viareggina*)	75
Apricot Fritters (*Bignè di albicocche*)	130
Tortellini with Vegetable and Shrimp Sauce	
(*Tortellini mare-orto*)	58
Red Mullet in Spicy Tomato Sauce (*Triglie alla livornese*)	76
Rocket Salad	—
Mixed Berry Fruits with Mascarpone*	

Vegetarian menus

Potato and Carrot Soup (*Minestra di patate e carote*)	46
Spinach-stuffed Pancakes (*Crespelle magre di spinaci*)	121
Pumpkin Pie (*Torta di zucca gialla*)	136
Baked Mozzarella (*Mozzarella al forno*)	34
Ribbon Pasta with Pesto (*Linguine al pesto genovese*)	64
Potato and Zucchini Omelet	
(*Frittata di patate e zucchini*)	121
Apricot Fritters (*Bignè di albicocche*)	130

*There are no recipes for simple dishes such as green salad or stewed fruits, where no page reference is indicated. Products marked with an * can be obtained from good Italian delicatessens and many large supermarkets.*

Glossary

This glossary is intended as a brief guide to some less familiar cookery terms and ingredients, including words and expressions found on Italian menus.

Abbacchio: spring lamb that has been fed exclusively on milk

Aceto balsamico: balsamic vinegar. Mild but highly aromatic, this wine-based vinegar, made in northern Italy, is traditionally matured for six to ten years in wooden casks.

Affogato: steamed or poached

Affumicato: smoked or cured

Aglio: garlic

Agnello: lamb that has been weaned

al dente: literally "to the tooth." The ideal consistency for cooked pasta, vegetables, and rice, tender but still firm to the bite.

Alchermes: red herbal liqueur based on cinnamon and flavored with cloves, coriander, and nutmeg

Amarene: small, sour cherries such as morello, the best variety for cooking

Amaretti: small, crisp almond cookies made from sweet and bitter almonds

Amaretto: almond liqueur, often used in dessert recipes

Amaro: bitter-tasting digestif liqueur, such as Fernet Branca

Arborio rice: Italian round-grained rice with a high starch content, particularly suitable for risottos

Arrosto: a meat roast

Baccalà: air-dried salt cod

Baste: to pour or spoon oil, fat, or liquid over food to prevent it from drying during cooking

Bel Paese: mild cow's milk cheese with a semi-soft, creamy texture

Biscottini: dry almond sponge finger cookies

Blanch: to plunge food into boiling water for a short period. This helps to remove strong flavors and softens vegetables before further cooking.

Bollito: boiled; boiled meats

Bresaola: air-dried salt beef, usually served in paper-thin slices

Brodetto: thick fish soup, found in various forms along the Adriatic coast

Burrata: high-fat buffalo's milk cheese

alla Cacciatore: "hunter style"; meat or fish cooked in a sauce that usually includes tomatoes, spring onions, mushrooms, bay leaves and wine

Cacciucco: a soup or stew containing a varied mixture of fish and shellfish, found along the Ligurian and Tuscan coasts

Caciocavallo: pear-shaped cow's milk cheese. Soft when fresh, the harder, more mature cheese is used for grating.

Caldo, molto caldo: warm, hot

Cannelloni: stuffed pasta rolls

Cannoli: small, crisp pastry rolls filled with ricotta or cream cheese, and often chocolate, pistachio and candiet fruit

Capocollo: loin or shoulder of pork, marinated in wine, air-dried and smoked

Chili peppers: hot red, yellow, or green members of the pepper family, used fresh or dried. They contain volatile oils that can irritate the skin and cause eyes to burn, and must be handled with caution. Wash hands immediately after using them.

Coppa: marinated, air-dried neck of pork, containing equal amounts of lean and fat

Cornmeal: In Italy, yellow cornmeal is used to make polenta, a staple of part of the north.

Cotechino: highly seasoned pork sausage

Coz.ze: mussels

Crostino: croûton, or small piece of toast, often served with different toppings as an appetizer

Crudo: raw

Dolce: sweet

Farcito: stuffed

Finocchiona: sausage similar to mortadella, strongly flavored with fennel

alla Fiorentina: literally "in the Florentine style"; usually means the dish is made with spinach

Fontina: medium-hard cheese similar to Gruyère, good for broiling or baking

Forno, al forno: baked

Freddo: cold

Fresco: fresh, uncooked

Frittata: omelet containing herbs, potatoes or other vegetables

Fritto misto: mixed fish and seafood, meat or vegetables fried in batter

Frutta: fruit

Frutti di mare: literally "fruit of the sea"; usually refers to a mixture of shellfish

Gelato: ice cream

Gnocchi: little pasta dumplings made with potatoes or semolina, sometimes flavored with spinach

Grana: generic term for hard cheeses with a brittle, grainy texture, such as Parmesan

Granita: flavored sorbet ice

Grappa: fiery alcoholic spirit distilled from the residues of grapes after pressing

Grissini: thin, crisp breadsticks

Insalata: salad

Lampascioni: rampions, slightly bitter onions used for pickling

Maraschino: liqueur made from maraschino cherries

alla marinara: "sailor style" sauce including tomato, garlic, oil, and oregano

Marinato: marinated

Mascarpone: a rich cream cheese, used in desserts and some pasta sauces

Mille foglie: flaky pastry – literally "a thousand leaves"

Minestra: light soup containing vegetables and pasta

Mortadella: large sausage, a specialty of Bologna, made from pork, diced bacon fat, pistachios, peppercorns, and garlic

Mostarda: candied fruit preserved in mustard syrup

Mozzarella: soft, white, mild cheese originally made from buffalo's milk, but now also made from cow's milk. Used particularly on pizzas and in salads

Pancetta: salted bacon, from the pig's belly, similar to slab bacon

Pan di Spagna: type of sponge cake used in desserts such as *Cassata alla siciliana* or *Zuppa inglese*

Pane: bread

Panettone: light yeast-raised cake containing candied fruits and yellow raisins. A version sold only at Eastertime, *Colomba pasquale*, is made in the shape of a dove.

Panforte: spicy Siennese cake including spices, almonds, and candied fruit

Panna: cream

Parmigiano reggiano: Parmesan. Hard yellow cheese, matured for at least a year. Ideal as a grating cheese, but also eaten as a table cheese when young.

Pasta: Italian staple made either from high-gluten flour, eggs, and butter or from semolina (durum wheat) and oil. There are numerous long and short varieties and shapes – for example, capeletti (hat-shaped), ditalini (small thimbles), farfalle (butterflies), conchiglie (shells), trenette (rippled flat strips), and stuffed agnolotti or tortellini. Pasta names as well as shapes can differ from region to region.

Pecorino: term for a number of hard yellow sheep cheeses, similar to Parmesan, but sharper

Peperoncini: fresh or dried hot red peppers

Pesto: paste of fresh basil, pine nuts, olive oil, garlic, and Parmesan cheese, served in soup or over pasta

Piadini: round, flat loaves baked on a hot earthenware slab

Pinzimonio: vegetable dip made from vinegar, olive oil, pepper, and salt

alla Pizzaiola: with a sauce of tomatoes, garlic, oregano, and black pepper

Polenta: northern Italian staple made from cornmeal, served plain or mixed with other ingredients and baked or fried

Prosciutto crudo: raw, unsmoked ham

Provola: soft cheese similar to mozzarella

Provolone: hard, cream-colored cheese. Its flavor ranges from mild to piquant, depending on the degree of maturity

Radicchio rosso: slightly bitter-flavored red chicory, used raw for winter salads and in cooking

Ragù: meat sauce

Render: to refine, or melt, the pure fat out of meat or poultry fat and tissues. Rendered fat, especially pork or goose, is used for cooking.

Ricotta: soft, mild, white cheese made from cow's or sheep's milk. Its bland but delicate flavor is suitable for both savory and sweet dishes.

Ripieno: stuffing; filled or stuffed

Robiola: small, rectangular cheese with a reddish rind, made from cow's or ewe's milk and best eaten young. Similar to tallegio cheese.

Rucola: rocket

Salamini: small pork sausages, often seasoned with peperoncini

Salsa: sauce

Salsiccia: fresh pork sausage

Scamorza: mild fresh or smoked cow's milk cheese

Secco: dry

Soppressata: lean, highly seasoned pork sausage

Spiedino: roasted on a spit or skewer

Spumante: generic term for sparkling wines, such as Asti Spumante, Lambrusco

Tallegio: square-shaped, strong-smelling cheese

Tartufi: truffles

Toma: strong-smelling cow's milk cheese made in blocks

in Umido: braised in a sauce of tomatoes and finely chopped vegetables

Vermouth: aperitif made from herbs and spices

Vialone rice: Italian round-grained rice, ideal for risotto

Zampone: highly spiced pork sausage encased in the skin of a pig's foot

Zuppa: thick soup: but Zuppa inglese is a rich custard dessert.

CONVERSION CHART

These figures are not exact equivalents, but have been rounded up or down slightly to make measuring easier.

Weight Equivalents		Volume Equivalents	
Metric	Imperial	Metric	Imperial
15 g	½ oz.	8 cl	3 fl. oz.
30 g	1 oz.	12,5 cl	4 fl. oz.
60 g	2 oz.	15 cl	¼ pint
90 g	3 oz.	17,5 cl	6 fl. oz.
125 g	¼ lb.	25 cl	8 fl. oz.
150 g	5 oz.	30 cl	½ pint
200 g	7 oz.	35 cl	12 fl. oz.
250 g	½ lb.	45 cl	¾ pint
350 g	¾ lb.	50 cl	16 fl. oz.
500 g	1 lb.	60 cl	1 pint
1 kg	2 to 2¼ lb.	1 liter	35 fl. oz.

Recipe Index

Cover: *Penne all'arrabbiata* – pasta with a sauce of mushrooms, bacon, garlic, tomatoes, and chili peppers (recipe, page 62) – makes a spicy appetizer, accompanied by a glass of Italian red wine. The buffalo's milk mozzarella cheese and ripe tomatoes, when combined with the black olives, fresh basil, and olive oil, will be transformed into *Mozzarella e pomodori* (recipe, page 34), served as an antipasto.

Published in the United States by
Thunder Bay Press
An imprint of the Advantage Publishers Group
5880 Oberlin Drive
San Diego, CA 92121-4794
www.advantagebooksonline.com

Published originally under the title
Küchen der Welt: Italien
© Copyright 1993 Gräfe und Unzer Verlag
GmbH, Munich

English translation for the US edition
© Copyright 1999 Gräfe und Unzer Verlag
GmbH, Munich
American adaptation by Josephine Bacon,
American Pie, London.

Library of Congress Cataloging-in-
Publication Data.
Alberti, Miranda.
Cuisines of the world: Italy / Miranda Alberti;
food photography, Michael Brauner. p. cm.
Includes index. ISBN 1-57145-257-5
I. Cookery, Italian. I. Title.
TX723 A4345 2000. 641.5945–dc21

1 2 3 4 5   00 01 02 03 04

Color reproduction by Fotolito Longo, Bolzano, Italy
Typeset by Satz + Litho Sporer KG, Augsburg, Germany
Printed and bound by Artes Gráficas Toledo S.A.U.
D.L.TO: 244-2000

GRÄFE UND UNZER

EDITORS: Dr Stefanie von Werz-Kovacs
and Birgit Rademacker
Sub-Editor: Monika Arndt
Designer: Konstantin Kern
Recipes tested by: Monika Arndt, Susanne
Bluhm, Doris Leitner, Doris Fahr-Scheu,
Ulrike Scheu, Gabi Scheu-Schmidt, Eva-
Maria Zehetmair
Production: Esta Denroche
Cartography: Huber, Munich

NORTH AMERICAN EDITION:
Managing Editor: JoAnn Padgett
Project Editor: Elizabeth McNulty

Miranda Alberti, the author, was born in Ferrara and grew up with traditional Italian cuisine. She is a philosophy graduate and a passionate cook. Many of the dishes in this book are her own family recipes passed down by word of mouth. Michael Brauner, who photographed the food for this volume, is a graduate of the Berlin Fotoschule. He worked as an assistant to several French and German photographers before setting up on his own in 1984. He now divides his time between his studios in Munich, Karlsruhe, and Gordes in Provence.

Kathrin Gaus studied graphic design in her home town of Braunschweig, and later moved to Munich. But the inspiration for her lively illustrations comes from her love of travel, and a special affinity with southern France and Italy.

Picture Credits

Color illustrations: Kathrin Gaus

All photographs were taken by Michael
Brauner, Food Fotografie, unless
indicated below:

Cover: Graham Kirk, London. 4 (beans
and squash blossoms, Italian market):
Erika Casparek-Türkkan, Bernried. 4-5:
top (man on donkey, Apulia) and bottom
right (boats, Cinque Terre), Martin Thomas,
Aachen-Alt Lemiers; middle (bar in Lucca),
Klaus D. Neumann, Munich. 89 (Venice):
Harald Mante, Dortmund. 10: Daniele
Messina, Mannheim. 11: top, ai aigner
impuls, Gottfried Aigner, Munich; bottom,
real bild Klaus D. Neumann, Munich.
1213: real bild Klaus D. Neumann, Munich.
1415, 16: Martin Thomas, Aachen-Alt
Lemiers. 17: top, real bild Klaus D.
Neumann, Munich; bottom, Martin Thomas,
Aachen-Alt Lemiers. 1819: K.
Wagenhäuser/jd Bildagentur, Munich. 19,
20, 21: Martin Thomas, Aachen-Alt
Lemiers. 22: top, real bild Klaus D.
Neumann, Munich; bottom, Martin Thomas,
Aachen-Alt Lemiers. 23, 24: Martin
Thomas, Aachen-Alt Lemiers. 25, 29: real
bild Klaus D. Neumann, Munich. 52:
Herbert Hartmann, Munich. 59, 65:
Fotostudio Teubner, Füssen. 78: Martin
Thomas, Aachen-Alt Lemiers. 90, 97:
Fotostudio Teubner, Füssen. 100: Hermann
Rademacker, Munich. 111: Erika Casparek-
Türkkan, Bernried.